Academic

Preparation

In Social Studies

Teaching for Transition
From High School
To College

College Entrance Examination Board, New York, 1986

Academic Preparation in Social Studies is one of a series of six books. The Academic Preparation Series includes books in English, the Arts, Mathematics, Science, Social Studies, and Foreign Language. Single copies of any one of these books can be purchased for $6.95. Orders for 5 through 49 copies of a single title receive a 20 percent discount; orders for 50 copies or more receive a 50 percent discount.

A boxed set of all the books in the Academic Preparation Series is available for $20. Orders for five or more sets receive a 20 percent discount. Each set also includes a copy of *Academic Preparation for College: What Students Need to Know and Be Able to Do.*

Payment or purchase order for individual titles or the set should be addressed to: College Board Publications, Box 886, New York, New York 10101.

The short story "Eveline" which appears in Appendix B and is discussed on pages 57–65 of the text, is reprinted by permission. Copyright 1916 by B.W. Huebsch; definitive text Copyright © 1967 by the Estate of James Joyce. James Joyce, *Dubliners* (New York: Viking Penguin, Inc., 1956), pp. 34–39.

Selected lines from "The King and I" by Richard Rodgers and Oscar Hammerstein II are reprinted by permission on pages 47 to 57. Copyright, 1951, by Richard Rodgers and Oscar Hammerstein II; Copyright in Canada, 1951, by Richard Rodgers and Oscar Hammerstein II. Musical compositions Copyrighted, 1951, by Richard Rodgers and Oscar Hammerstein II. Taken from *6 Plays by Rodgers and Hammerstein* (New York: The Modern Library, 1959).

ISBN: 0-87447-224-5

9 8 7 6 5 4 3 2 1

Contents

Contents

Contributing Writer and Principal Consultant

James A. Banks, Professor and Chairman, Curriculum and Instruction, University of Washington, Seattle

History and Social Sciences Advisory Committee, 1984-85

Fay D. Metcalf, History Coordinator/Teacher, Boulder High School, Colorado *(Chair)*

Mildred Alpern, History Teacher, Spring Valley Senior High School, New York

Donald R. Come, Professor of Social Science and Assistant Dean for Academic Affairs, Michigan State University, East Lansing

Martha H. Gay, Social Science Teacher, Benjamin Elijah Mays High School, Atlanta, Georgia

John R. Howe, Professor of History and American Studies, University of Minnesota, Minneapolis

Helen M. Redbird, Professor of Social Science, Western Oregon State College, Monmouth

John O. Voll, Professor of History, University of New Hampshire, Durham

Acknowledgments

The College Board wishes to thank all the individuals and organizations that contributed to *Academic Preparation in Social Studies.* In addition to those who served on the History and Social Sciences Advisory Committee and the Council on Academic Affairs, explicit acknowledgment should be accorded to Barbara Martinsons, Yola Coffeen, Mary Carroll Scott, and Carol J. Meyer. Without the leadership of Peter Stearns of Carnegie-Mellon University and Adrienne Y. Bailey, Vice President for Academic Affairs at the College Board, this book would not have assumed its present form. Collaborating with Robert Orrill in the making of this book has been my own intellectual pleasure. Although none of these people individually is responsible for the contents of the book, the Educational EQuality Project owes much to their efforts.

James Herbert, General Editor

The College Board is a nonprofit membership organization that provides tests and other educational services for students, schools, and colleges. The membership is composed of more than 2,500 colleges, schools, school systems, and education associations. Representatives of the members serve on the Board of Trustees and advisory councils and committees that consider the College Board's programs and participate in the determination of its policies and activities.

The Educational EQuality Project is a 10-year effort of the College Board to strengthen the academic quality of secondary education and to ensure equality of opportunity for postsecondary education for all students. Begun in 1980, the project is under the direction of the Board's Office of Academic Affairs.

For more information about the Educational EQuality Project and inquiries about this book, write to the Office of Academic Affairs, The College Board, 45 Columbus Avenue, New York, New York 10023-6917.

To Our Fellow Teachers of History and Social Sciences

Teachers, like students, enjoy learning from one another, and one purpose of this book is to encourage the kind of discussion among teachers that can result in such learning. In preparing this book we talked to many colleagues and profited from their ideas about how to prepare students for college in history and social sciences. We heard particularly of their special concern for students regarded as being "at risk"—that is, those students in danger of narrowing their chances in life and work if they do not engage more fully with learning in school. We heard also that it is not always easy to identify those students who have potential, but not yet purpose and commitment. Moreover, we understand that problems can arise when some students in a class are set apart from others. The aim is to open the future for more students, not to predict too early those who will succeed and those who may not.

In this uncertainty, we believe the best approach is to emphasize the importance of the work that all share in the classroom and to make plain that we have high expectations of all students in their everyday efforts. This, as it happens, is fully consistent with the knowledge about past and present that we ask students to consider. American history and social science have always concerned themselves with the vitality, the fecundity, of the democratic experience. Just now, as a result of new inquiries in our field, we know in more vivid detail than ever before about the historical experiences of ordinary people. These experiences, we see, are full of aspiration and drama, and are anything but humdrum. In a recent book the historian Peter Gay gives us an epigraph that speaks to this awareness:

1

An ample theme: the intense interests, passions, and strategy that throb
through the commonest lives.
                                    —*Thomas Hardy, note of May 1882*[1]

In this book we discuss how history and social science teachers are
exploring this "ample theme" in new ways and what such activity
suggests for taking a fresh look at curriculum and instruction. The
suggestions we present, then, emerge directly from the current
work of teachers, not from a particular theory of learning. Moreover,
our intent is not to legislate the ideas presented, but rather to make
them available for the consideration of teachers as they discuss
how to strengthen history and social sciences in their local schools.
We seek, that is, to encourage and inform discussion, not to prescribe its specific results.

We believe that discussion and critical questioning also should
characterize the work of the classroom. This, too, is consistent with
the endeavors of historians and social scientists. The best work in
our field displays little dogmatism, but instead reveals a spirited
seeking after what we know can be elusive understanding. In the
book cited above, Peter Gay mentions how a much-studied historical subject still continues to be "awash with questions unanswered
and, for that matter, questions unasked."[2] Such is the case with
most topics we ask high school students to consider, and teachers
do well when they encourage *all* students to share in these questions. In this way we do fuller justice both to our subject matter
and to the fact that the learning of students often springs first from
puzzlement or perplexity, from their intuition for the "questions
unasked."

Social Studies Advisory Committee

---

1. In Peter Gay, *The Bourgeois Experience: Victoria to Freud*, vol. 1, *Education
of the Senses* (New York: Oxford University Press, 1984), p. ix.
2. Ibid., p. 9.

I. Beyond the Green Book

Identifying the academic preparation needed for college is a first step toward providing that preparation for all students who might aspire to higher education. But the real work of actually achieving these learning outcomes lies ahead.[1]

This book is a sequel to *Academic Preparation for College: What Students Need to Know and Be Able to Do*, which was published in 1983 by the College Board's Educational EQuality Project. Now widely known as the Green Book, *Academic Preparation for College* outlined the knowledge and skills students need in order to have a fair chance at succeeding in college. It summarized the combined judgments of hundreds of educators in every part of the country. The Green Book sketched learning outcomes that could serve as goals for high school curricula in six Basic Academic Subjects: English, the arts, mathematics, science, social studies, and foreign languages. It also identified six Basic Academic Competencies on which depend, and which are further developed by, work in these subjects. Those competencies are reading, writing, speaking and listening, mathematics, reasoning, and studying. The Green Book also called attention to additional competencies in using computers and observing, whose value to the college entrant increasingly is being appreciated.

With this book we take a step beyond *Academic Preparation for College*. The Green Book simply outlined desired results of high school education—the learning all students need to be adequately prepared for college. It contained no specific suggestions about how to achieve those results. Those of us working with the Educational EQuality Project strongly believed—and still believe—that ulti-

---

1. The College Board, *Academic Preparation for College: What Students Need to Know and Be Able to Do* (New York: The College Board, 1983), p. 31.

mately curriculum and instruction are matters of local expertise and responsibility. Building consensus on goals, while leaving flexible the means to achieve them, makes the most of educators' ability to respond appropriately and creatively to conditions in their own schools. Nevertheless, teachers and administrators, particularly those closely associated with the EQuality project, often have asked how the outcomes sketched in the Green Book might be translated into actual curricula and instructional practices—how they can get on with the "real work" of education. These requests in part seek suggestions about how the Green Book goals might be achieved; perhaps to an even greater extent they express a desire to get a fuller picture of those very briefly stated goals. Educators prefer to think realistically, in terms of courses and lessons. Discussion of proposals such as those in the Green Book proceeds more readily when goals are filled out and cast into the practical language of possible courses of action.

To respond to these requests for greater detail, and to encourage further nationwide discussion about what should be happening in our high school classrooms, teachers working with the Educational EQuality Project have prepared this book and five like it, one in each of the Basic Academic Subjects. By providing suggestions about how the outcomes described in *Academic Preparation for College* might be achieved, we hope to add more color and texture to the sketches in that earlier publication. We do not mean these suggestions to be prescriptive or definitive, but to spark more detailed discussion and ongoing dialogue among our fellow teachers who have the front-line responsibility for ensuring that all students are prepared adequately for college. We also intend this book and its companions for guidance counselors, principals, superintendents, and other officials who must understand the work of high school teachers if they are better to support and cooperate with them.

Students at Risk, Nation at Risk

Academic Preparation for College was the result of an extensive grassroots effort involving hundreds of educators in every part of the country. However, it was not published in a vacuum. Since the beginning of this decade, many blue-ribbon commissions and studies also have focused attention on secondary education. The concerns of these reports have been twofold. One, the reports note a perceptible decline in the academic attainments of students who graduate from high school, as indicated by such means as standardized test scores and comments from employers; two, the reports reflect a widespread worry that, unless students are better educated, our national welfare will be in jeopardy. *A Nation at Risk* made this point quite bluntly:

> Our Nation is at risk. Our once unchallenged preeminence in commerce, industry, science, and technological innovation is being overtaken by competitors throughout the world. . . . The educational foundations of our society are presently being eroded by a rising tide of mediocrity that threatens our very future as a Nation and a people.[2]

The Educational EQuality Project, an effort of the College Board throughout the decade of the 1980s to improve both the quality of preparation for college and the equality of access to it, sees another aspect of risk: if our nation is at risk because of the level of students' educational attainment, then we must be more concerned with those students who have been most at risk.

Overall, the predominance of the young in our society is ending. In 1981, as the EQuality project was getting under way, about 41 percent of our country's population was under 25 years old and 26 percent was 50 years old or older. By the year 2000, however, the balance will have shifted to 34 percent and 28 percent, respectively. But these figures do not tell the whole story, especially for those of us working in the schools. Among certain groups, youth is a growing segment of the population. For example, in 1981, 71 percent of black and 75 percent of Hispanic households had children 18 years old or younger. In comparison, only 52 percent of all white households had children in that age category. At the beginning of the 1980s, children from minority groups already made up more than

---

2. National Commission on Excellence in Education, *A Nation at Risk* (Washington, D.C.: U.S. Government Printing Office, 1983), p. 5.

25 percent of all public school students.[3] Clearly, concern for improving the educational attainments of all students increasingly must involve concern for students from such groups of historically disadvantaged Americans.

How well will such young people be educated? In a careful and thoughtful study of schools, John Goodlad found that "consistent with the findings of virtually every study that has considered the distribution of poor and minority students . . . minority students were found in disproportionately large percentages in the low track classes of the multiracial samples [of the schools studied]."[4] The teaching and learning that occur in many such courses can be disappointing in comparison to that occurring in other courses. Goodlad reported that in many such courses very little is expected, and very little is attempted.[5]

When such students are at risk, the nation itself is at risk, not only economically but morally. That is why this book and its five companions offer suggestions that will be useful in achieving academic excellence for *all* students. We have attempted to take into account that the resources of some high schools may be limited and that some beginning high school students may not be well prepared. We have tried to identify ways to keep open the option of preparing adequately for college as late as possible in the high school years. These books are intended for work with the broad spectrum of high school students—not just a few students and not only those currently in the "academic track." We are convinced that many more students can—and, in justice, should—profit from higher education and therefore from adequate academic preparation.

Moreover, many more students actually enroll in postsecondary education than currently follow the "academic track" in high school. Further, discussions with employers have emphasized that many of the same academic competencies needed by college-bound

3. Ernest L. Boyer, *High School* (New York: Harper & Row, 1983), pp. 4-5. U.S. Department of Education, National Center for Education Statistics, *Digest of Education Statistics: 1982* (Washington, D.C.: U.S. Government Printing Office, 1982), p. 43.

4. John Goodlad, *A Place Called School* (New York: McGraw-Hill, 1984), p. 156.

5. Ibid., p. 159.

students also are needed by high school students going directly into the world of work. Consequently, the Educational EQuality Project, as its name indicates, hopes to contribute to achieving a democratic excellence in our high schools.

The Classroom: At the Beginning as Well as the End of Improvement

A small book such as this one, intended only to stimulate dialogue about what happens in the classroom, cannot address all the problems of secondary education. On the other hand, we believe that teachers and the actual work of education—that is to say, curriculum and instruction—should be a more prominent part of the nationwide discussion about improving secondary education.

A 1984 report by the Education Commission of the States found that 44 states either had raised high school graduation requirements or had such changes pending. Twenty-seven states had enacted new policies dealing with instructional time, such as new extracurricular policies and reduced class sizes.[6] This activity reflects the momentum for and concern about reform that has been generated recently. It demonstrates a widespread recognition that critiques of education without concrete proposals for change will not serve the cause of improvement. But what will such changes actually mean in the classroom? New course requirements do not necessarily deal with the academic quality of the courses used to fulfill those requirements. Certain other kinds of requirements can force instruction to focus on the rote acquisition of information to the exclusion of fuller intellectual development. Manifestly, juggling of requirements and courses without attention to what needs to occur between teachers and students inside the classroom will not automatically produce better prepared students. One proponent of reform, Ernest Boyer, has noted that there is danger in the prevalence of "quick-fix" responses to the call for improvement. "The depth of discussion

6. *Action in the States: Progress toward Education Renewal,* A Report by the Task Force on Education for Economic Growth (Denver, Colorado: Education Commission of the States, 1984), p. 27.

about the curriculum . . . has not led to a serious and creative look at the nature of the curriculum. . . . states [have not asked] what we ought to be teaching."[7]

Such questioning and discussion is overdue. Clearly, many improvements in secondary education require action outside the classroom and the school. Equally clearly, even this action should be geared to a richer, more developed understanding of what is needed in the classroom. By publishing these books we hope to add balance to the national debate about improving high school education. Our point is not only that it is what happens between teachers and students in the classroom that makes the difference. Our point is also that what teachers and students do in classrooms must be thoughtfully considered before many kinds of changes, even exterior changes, are made in the name of educational improvement.

From Deficit to Development

What we can do in the classroom is limited, of course, by other factors. Students must be there to benefit from what happens in class. Teachers know firsthand that far too many young people of high school age are no longer even enrolled. Nationally, the drop-out rate in 1980 among the high school population aged 14 to 34 was 13 percent. It was higher among low-income and minority students. Nearly 1 out of 10 high schools had a drop-out rate of over 20 percent.[8]

Even when students stay in high school, we know that they do not always have access to the academic preparation they need. Many do not take enough of the right kinds of courses. In 1980, in almost half of all high schools, a majority of the students in each of those schools was enrolled in the "general" curriculum. Nationwide, only 38 percent of high school seniors had been in an academic program; another 36 percent had been in a general program;

---

7. In Thomas Toch, "For School Reform's Top Salesmen, It's Been Some Year," *Education Week*, June 6, 1984, p. 33.

8. National Center for Education Statistics, *Digest of Education Statistics: 1982*, p. 68. Donald A. Rock et al., "Factors Associated with Test Score Decline: Briefing Paper" (Princeton, New Jersey: Educational Testing Service, December 1984), p. 4.

and 24 percent had followed a vocational/technical track. Only 39 percent of these seniors had enrolled for three or more years in history or social studies; only 33 percent had taken three or more years of mathematics; barely 22 percent had taken three or more years of science; and less than 8 percent of these students had studied Spanish, French, or German for three or more years.[9]

Better than anyone else, teachers know that, even when students are in high school and are enrolled in the needed academic courses, they must attend class regularly. Yet some school systems report daily absence rates as high as 20 percent. When 1 out of 5 students enrolled in a course is not actually there, it is difficult even to begin carrying out a sustained, coherent program of academic preparation.

As teachers we know that such problems cannot be solved solely by our efforts in the classroom. In a world of disrupted family and community structures; economic hardship; and rising teenage pregnancy, alcoholism, and suicide, it would be foolish to believe that attention to curriculum and instruction can remedy all the problems leading to students' leaving high school, taking the wrong courses, and missing classes. Nonetheless, what happens in the high school classroom—once students are there—is important in preparing students not only for further education but for life.

Moreover, as teachers, we also hope that what happens in the classroom at least can help students stick with their academic work. Students may be increasingly receptive to this view. In 1980 more than 70 percent of high school seniors wanted greater academic emphasis in their schools; this was true of students in all curricula. Mortimer Adler may have described a great opportunity:

> There is little joy in most of the learning they [students] are now compelled to do. Too much of it is make-believe, in which neither teacher nor pupil can take a lively interest. Without some joy in learning—a joy that arises from hard work well done and from the participation of one's mind in a common task—basic schooling cannot initiate the young into the life of learning, let alone give them the skill and the incentive to engage in it further.[10]

---

9. National Center for Education Statistics, *Digest of Education Statistics: 1982*, p. 70.

10. Mortimer J. Adler, *The Paideia Proposal: An Educational Manifesto* (New York: Macmillan Publishing Company, 1982), p. 32.

Genuine academic work can contribute to student motivation and persistence. Goodlad's study argues strongly that the widespread focus on the rote mechanics of a subject is a surefire way to distance students from it or to ensure that they do not comprehend all that they are capable of understanding. Students need to be encouraged to become inquiring, involved learners. It is worth trying to find more and better ways to engage them actively in the learning process, to build on their strengths and enthusiasms. Consequently, the approaches suggested in these books try to shift attention from chronicling what students do not know toward developing the full intellectual attainments of which they are capable and which they will need in college.

Dimensions for a Continuing Dialogue

This book and its five companions were prepared during 1984 and 1985 under the aegis of the College Board's Academic Advisory Committees. Although each committee focused on the particular issues facing its subject, the committees had common purposes and common approaches. Those purposes and approaches may help give shape to the discussion that this book and its companions hope to stimulate.

Each committee sought the assistance of distinguished writers and consultants. The committees considered suggestions made in the dialogues that preceded and contributed to *Academic Preparation for College* and called on guest colleagues for further suggestions and insights. Each committee tried to take account of the best available thinking and research but did not merely pass along the results of research or experience. Each deliberated about those findings and then tried to suggest approaches that had actually worked to achieve learning outcomes described in *Academic Preparation for College*. The suggestions in these books are based to a great extent on actual, successful high school programs.

These books focus not only on achieving the outcomes for a particular subject described in the Green Book but also on how study of that subject can develop the Basic Academic Competencies. The learning special to each subject has a central role to play in preparing students for successful work in college. That role ought not to be neglected in a rush to equip students with more general skills. It is learning in a subject that can engage a student's interest, activity, and commitment. Students do, after all, read about *something*, write about *something*, reason about *something*. We thought it important to suggest that developing the Basic Academic Competencies does not replace, but can result from, mastering the unique knowledge and skills of each Basic Academic Subject. Students, particularly hungry and undernourished ones, should not be asked to master the use of the fork, knife, and spoon without being served an appetizing, full, and nourishing meal.

In preparing the book for each subject, we also tried to keep in mind the connections among the Basic Academic Subjects. For example, the teaching of English and the other languages should build on students' natural linguistic appetite and development— and this lesson may apply to the teaching of other subjects as well. The teaching of history with emphasis on the full range of human experience, as approached through both social and global history, bears on the issue of broadening the "canon" of respected works in literature and the arts. The teaching of social studies, like the teaching of science, involves mathematics not only as a tool but as a mode of thought. There is much more to make explicit and to explore in such connections among the Basic Academic Subjects. Teachers may teach in separate departments, but students' thought is probably not divided in the same way.

Finally, the suggestions advanced here generally identify alternate ways of working toward the same outcomes. We wanted very much to avoid any hint that there is one and only one way to achieve the outcomes described in *Academic Preparation for College*. There are many good ways of achieving the desired results, each one good in its own way and in particular circumstances. By describing alternate approaches, we hope to encourage readers of this book to analyze and recombine alternatives and to create the most appropriate and effective approaches, given their own particular situations.

We think that this book and its five companion volumes can be useful to many people. Individual teachers may discover suggestions that will spur their own thought about what might be done in the classroom; small groups of teachers may find the book useful in reconsidering the social studies program in their high school. It also may provide a takeoff point for in-service sessions. Teachers in several subjects might use it and its companions to explore concerns, such as the Basic Academic Competencies, that range across the high school curriculum. Principals may find these volumes useful in refreshing the knowledge and understanding on which their own instructional leadership is based.

We also hope that these books will prove useful to committees of teachers and officials in local school districts and at the state level who are examining the high school curriculum established in their jurisdictions. Public officials whose decisions directly or indirectly affect the conditions under which teaching and learning occur may find in the books an instructive glimpse of the kinds of things that should be made possible in the classroom.

Colleges and universities may find in all six books occasion to consider not only how they are preparing future teachers, but also whether their own curricula will be suited to students receiving the kinds of preparation these books suggest. But our greatest hope is that this book and its companions will be used as reference points for dialogues between high school and college teachers. It was from such dialogues that *Academic Preparation for College* emerged. We believe that further discussions of this sort can provide a wellspring of insight and energy to move beyond the Green Book toward actually providing the knowledge and skills all students need to be successful in college.

We understand the limitations of the suggestions presented here. Concerning what happens in the classroom, many teachers, researchers, and professional associations can speak with far greater depth and detail than is possible in the pages that follow. This book aspires only to get that conversation going, particularly across the boundaries that usually divide those concerned about education, and especially as it concerns the students who often are least well served. Curriculum, teaching, and learning are far too central to be omitted from the discussion about improving education.

II. The Outcomes and Organizing the Body of Knowledge

In this book we suggest that the social studies curriculum should be augmented and refined by taking into account new findings in social history, by adopting a worldwide perspective, and by incorporating social science concepts more thoroughly. These suggestions are based on current thought in history and the social sciences—advances that have made history in particular a vital field of learning in recent years. We believe that the modifications suggested here can help make social studies a rewarding subject for a wider range of students and can help many of these students succeed in college.

These suggestions involve rethinking and, to some extent, reorganizing the body of knowledge presented in the social studies curriculum. But throughout we have tried to bear in mind the actual contexts in which any such action takes place. We know that communities expect many things of their social studies curriculum in addition to the academic core we see as necessary preparation for college. We know, for example, that in most communities, established policy requires certain social studies courses: American history, American government, and in many cases world history. Furthermore, we recognize that different communities wish different emphases within courses so that one may want special attention given to rural life, while another may wish to have life in a particular region stressed. In this book, therefore, we attempt to suggest opportunities for curriculum modification that are flexible enough to fit into the actual context of the current social studies curriculum.

Moreover, our suggestions build upon what many social studies teachers already are beginning to do. We know that greater attention to social history, to a worldwide perspective, and to social science concepts requires that both room and resources be found for these new emphases. In many cases, however, teachers find that the perspectives and concepts involved in these new approaches can provide ways to reorganize existing content and thereby increase opportunities to integrate other material. Moreover, we have tried to make suggestions that are consistent with existing textbooks, knowing full well that teachers make use of textbooks for many constructive purposes when they organize content and material to be studied.

As history and social science teachers we believe that by taking seriously the kinds of questions our disciplines have taught us to ask and try to answer, we can and should be causes of change in the curriculum, rather than passive recipients of such change. Take, for example, the problem of the overload of detailed information. A worldwide perspective requires that historians look for large-scale periodizations and comparative analyses of institutions and developments. The history of the world simply cannot be comprehended ruler by ruler, battle by battle, event by event. Similarly, social historians try to identify the large processes and transformations at work in specific situations and events. Such general understandings give order, context, and meaning to particulars. The organization of curriculum, that is, can benefit from understandings inherent in our own skills and material, and such understandings after all are more to the point than mechanical rearrangements of units of study.

Or consider the long-standing but sometimes awkward alliance of history and the social sciences under the rubric of social studies. The new emphases perhaps point toward a more meaningful partnership. Social history, for example, illustrates that history itself has been transformed by the emergence and use of social science questions, concepts, and knowledge. This transformation brings the possibility of greater coherence to the social studies curriculum. New concepts that have provided important organizing questions in history courses may be built upon, elaborated, and developed further in various social science courses. Alternately, concepts introduced in social science courses may be assumed and elaborated in history courses, thereby allowing richer and more sophisticated characterizations, explanations, and interpretations of the past.

In short, we believe that the present moment holds much opportunity for the social studies curriculum. By calling upon the kinds of inquiry proper to history and the social sciences, and particularly to recent advances in those fields, social studies teachers can bring new perspectives to the organization of curriculum. These perspectives, we believe, can bring deeper meaning and interest, as well as greater coherence and comprehensibility, to the social studies curriculum. But we do not propose a new curriculum. What follows in this chapter is, instead, a commentary teachers should find useful as they consider curricular frameworks. We hope that the thoughts presented here will stimulate our colleagues to think further and deeper as they work to organize study in their local schools and settings. We propose some places to begin and some things to consider, but do not prescribe a final result.

Sequence and Scope

The suggestions in this chapter are meant to elaborate the social studies content outcomes in *Academic Preparation for College*; they also provide the context within which to consider the skills outcomes discussed in Chapter 3 of this book. (For convenient reference, we reprint the complete outcomes statement in social studies in Appendix A.) They can be translated into curricular plans in many ways. For convenience of discussion we assume a set of courses—World History, United States History, and American Government—familiar in many localities. We believe that these usual, and in many places required, courses can be built into an academic core for the social studies curriculum. This academic core could provide the history and social science learning students need to do well in college. At the same time, it would allow for other courses that local districts, schools, or teachers might find desirable for their particular students. This flexibility is multiplied if curricular planners think in terms of the entire secondary school curriculum extending from grade 7 to grade 12. And indeed, sound curricular planning will want to take into account the entire pattern of opportunities available in the secondary school curriculum. Our intent here is more modest. We focus only on an academic core that might be presented in senior high school, and do not address directly the matters of prior or elective courses.

The traditional approach to thinking about social studies curriculum has been by the creation of scope and sequence plans. Defining scope involves identifying the content or topics that will be treated in social studies courses; deciding sequence involves laying out the order in which topics and experiences will be presented in such courses. Moreover, there are some fairly common strategies by which scope and sequence plans are generally worked out: the chronological, the topical, the area studies, and the conceptual. Most social studies curricula probably employ a combination or blend of these strategies. In this chapter we address each strategy only indirectly, keeping primary attention on questions related to the three large curricular suggestions we have presented, which were stated at the beginning of the chapter.

Sequence and Integration

The first such question we address is that of curricular integration, and so turn to the matter of sequence before taking up the question of scope. In thinking about sequence in the social studies curriculum the dimension of historical chronology comes most readily to mind. But it is important to remember that the order of past events and developments is not the only dimension of time in the social studies curriculum. Students' intellectual development also follows its own pattern: the elaboration of concepts proceeds from elementary grasp to more complex use, and certain class activities appropriate to these different times of intellectual development and conceptual unfolding themselves take shorter or longer periods of time. Time in the social studies curriculum thus cannot be organized simply by scaling down the sequence of events and developments in the past.

Nonetheless, chronology is an essential organizing principle in the study of history. Without some understanding of earlier traditional societies, students cannot proceed to an understanding of modern societies. Without some understanding of the proportion of Americans living on farms before 1870, for example, urbanization cannot be seen as a change that calls for explanation. The problem of change over time simply will not be posed. However, chronology is not necessarily a matter of recounting a sequence of individual actions and events such as we might find in a chronicle. This is the approach that sometimes bogs down history courses. Instead, continuity and change over time can be organized and presented at varying levels of generality. Historians routinely use concepts of period and process, for example, as well as ones more directly associated with the social sciences, to organize the sequence of past events and developments. Such concepts can provide a manageable chronological frame within which more tangible occurrences can be located and investigated.

A sequence suggested by chronology can be coordinated with progressive refinement of the historical skills described in Chapter 3. World history provides ample opportunities to develop students' ability to recognize continuity, change, and turning points in history. One text, for example, leads students into the following line of thought: "Discuss the differences between Hinduism and Buddhism. How does the Moslem faith differ from Hinduism and Buddhism? How did the division between Hindus and Moslems make it easier for the British to control India? Why were the Moslems less eager than the Hindus to drive out the British? What is the situation today?" In responding to such questions students may construct a large-scale and useful chronological sequence while practicing their abilities to recognize continuity and change over time.

Later course work could emphasize the more complex intellectual skills of inquiring into cause and effect. Students who learned to regard seventeenth-century English migration to North America as largely a matter of religious differences may come to see the operation of multiple factors including population pressure, demand for labor, and the immigrants' own vision of the United States as contributing causes in the early twentieth-century migrations to the United States. This intellectual development may even lead students to suggest varying causal interpretations as suggested in Chapter 3. Were religious differences still a cause of immigration in the twentieth century? In many cases students can test such a hypothesis on the basis of information in their own textbooks.

Sequence in the social studies curriculum also provides opportunity to develop greater sophistication in the use of specific concepts. If students have made progress in sharpening the distinction between agrarian and industrial societies, then exploring the period from 1780 to 1870 in United States history will provide a chance to see industrialization as a gradual process advanced by some factors in a society, resisted by others. One textbook describes this unfolding process by introducing questions of location, inventiveness, labor, and financing as they come to the fore in United States history. By drawing these accounts together, students will not only develop an integrated sense of the process of industrialization, but will also acquire a repertoire of concepts that might be further developed in an economics course.

In Chapter 4 we suggest some teaching exercises that can provide practice in the development of intellectual skills and in the elaboration of concepts. The time that such exercises require is another consideration in planning sequence in the social studies curriculum. Our point here is not to recommend one specific sequence, but to indicate that developing an integrated social studies curriculum is not only needed but possible and that integration has several dimensions. Managing time in the social studies curriculum involves chronology, students' intellectual development, the elaboration of concepts, and the time needed for appropriate exercises. Whatever curricular sequence a high school offers, it should "hang together" in a coherent way.

Scope and Selection

The sketch of needed learning outcomes in social studies presented in *Academic Preparation for College* begins with four general or umbrella statements that provide an orientation to the more specific content goals stated in the sections devoted to world history, United States history, and social science. Those four statements are:

- Basic factual knowledge of major political and economic institutions and their historical development.
- Basic factual knowledge of the social and cultural fields of history.
- An introductory knowledge of the content and concepts of the social sciences.
- A grasp of major trends in the contemporary world (for example, nationalism or urbanization).

In combining knowledge of social history with the more usual knowledge of the history of political and economic institutions, *Academic Preparation for College* suggests that the past is best understood in the round. Such understanding involves some sense of all the participants in a society and all the aspects of their life. Family and community life, how children are raised and educated, what work people do and the circumstances in which they do it, are aspects of the past that need to be incorporated into the study of history. Understanding of the past is distorted when limited to the rise of nation-states or successive occupants of the presidency. Nor can history be limited to the most sublime intellectual and artistic "contributions" of a civilization. Instead, it involves the whole way of life of a civilization: the customs of a people, their typical patterns of action, their values, and their arts.

Understanding these aspects of the human past has grown enormously in the last 25 years, and in the incorporation of these bodies of knowledge lies what we regard as the promise of social history. High school students will have the opportunity to investigate and understand people and activities less distant from themselves. This is particularly true of minority and female students. Until recently, members of these groups have seldom had the opportunity to become kings or congressmen, captains of armies or of industry. But social history comes closer to all students. The histories that students are living are set more in the family, the schools, and the community than in the corridors of political and military power.

United States History

Inclusion of knowledge drawn from social history is important to the whole of the social studies curriculum but is nowhere more critical than in the United States history course. Here there is clear need to bring the school history classroom in closer touch with new energies of historical inquiry. Michael Kammen observes that the guild of American historians "is undergoing the most creative ferment in its entire lifetime"[1] and adds that this intense activity is most evident in "the steady expansion of the reach of social his-

---

1. Michael Kammen (ed.), "Introduction: The Historian's Vocation and the State of the Discipline in the United States," in *The Past Before Us: Contemporary Historical Writing in the United States* (Ithaca, New York: Cornell University Press, 1980), p. 22.

19

tory."[2] Some of this ferment must also stir in our classrooms if students are to become aware of and prepare to take advantage of the learning opportunities in history that await them in college.

Here we have an opportunity to help the study of history become more inward for students. We noted that explorations in social history can be more various, and sometimes more personally meaningful, to students than accounts restricted largely to politics and wars. Samuel Johnson once remarked that accounts of history seldom descend "below the consultation of senates, the motions of armies, and the schemes of conspirators."[3] These are matters, he noted, very distant from the lives of most people (himself included); they are matters "which we think ourselves never likely to feel, and with which we have never yet been acquainted."[4] But social history, with American historians in its forefront, has much enlarged our angle of vision on the past and in so doing has included much more of human experience within historical knowledge. It looks at the past, in a memorable phrase, "from the bottom up"— that is, from the locations of ordinary people in everyday structures of life. By including this vantage point in study, we can draw attention to ordinary features of life like family and gender as products of historical change, and bring to bear historical understanding on experiences common to most students.

Social history, however, does not in itself provide a comprehensive scheme or strategy for organizing the United States history course. Its findings, while illuminating, have not yet resulted in a large synthesis of American history or a tidy new scheme of periodization. Their import, instead, has been to increase greatly the amount and variety of topics open to historical study and, as a result, to expand and stimulate historical consciousness. As Robert Darnton says, the main thrust of social history at present is "not to reconstruct a single past but to burrow in different directions."[5]

---

2. Ibid., p. 34.

3. "Samuel Johnson." In James L. Clifford (ed.), *Biography as an Art: Selected Criticism 1560-1960* (New York: Oxford University Press, 1962), p. 41.

4. Ibid., p. 40.

5. Robert Darnton, "Intellectual and Cultural History." In Kammen, op. cit., p. 329.

These new paths open in many directions—not only to those mentioned before, but also toward historical studies of such experiences as youth and aging, work and leisure, health and illness. We also can add many others such as race, ethnicity, and religion. That we do not know where all these possibilities may lead can be a stimulus to curiosity and study. By selecting some for exploration, teachers help students recognize that history is not simply a much-repeated story known by its familiar events and predictable conclusions. That is, students begin to know history as inquiry, as an active rethinking of the past.

Moreover, topics from social history selected for their particular interest or importance need not conflict with, or be taken up in isolation from, the patterns of familiar political and economic chronologies. In Chapter 3 we discuss how one such choice, the study of migration, relates to the larger account of American history. The history of how one group of people came to the United States, found or didn't find work, and made lives for themselves inevitably interacts with the stories of the other peoples of the United States. Moreover, this study can be linked readily with the important points in the political account. Immigration, for example, had much to do with developments such as the realignment of political parties before the Civil War and the emergence of "machine" politics in cities later in the nineteenth century. Indeed, our politics at all levels cannot be understood unless we ask how new Americans used the political process or found it used against them.

As we integrate social history with traditional political accounts, we begin to move toward a more comprehensive vision of the American past. This is in the interest of accuracy and also meets better the educational needs and interests of a diverse population like that of the United States. Students of all cultural and ethnic groups need to see their history mirrored in school history. Too often in the past women, working people, and ethnic and racial minorities— among them Native Americans, Hispanics, and blacks—have seen little of their historical experience reflected in study. Social history gives attention to these groups and others that usually have been left out of historical accounts, including, as Darnton puts it, "the oppressed, the inarticulate, the marginal."[6] In so doing, it gives a

---

6. Ibid.

more complete picture of our political past. Earlier, for example, most historians and social scientists tended to emphasize the pursuit and exercise of power in their studies of politics. The newer approach to inquiry, by contrast, adds increased understanding about *responses* to structures of power, including the efforts of minority and oppressed groups to retain a vital cohesion despite the opposition they met. This more inclusive view, as Kammen says, results in historical inquiry that is "more responsive to the pluralistic and increasingly egalitarian society in which it functions."[7]

World History, Geography, and Cultures

Nowhere is the problem of "coverage" more daunting to the history teacher than in the area of world history. Even those teachers who sail with some assurance into the several hundred years of United States history or the many more centuries of European history pause in more than a little perplexity before the seven- or eight-thousand-year history of human civilization on this planet. Consequently, the content learning outcomes listed in *Academic Preparation for College* for the area of World History, Geography, and Cultures need to be understood as much as principles of selection as definitions of scope.

We want to emphasize that the topic here is the *world*, not each and every one of its constituent parts. The focus is on developments that are of the largest significance to the whole of civilization. Historians build up knowledge of the past inductively, bit by bit, particular fact by particular fact. But teaching about the history of the world must proceed from the top down, deductively, employing ways in which the events and developments of the past can be grouped together as commonalities, continuities, and contrasts. From this point of view, the movement from traditional to modern societies, the spread of the most widely shared religions and languages, and the still developing worldwide shift to industrial economies are the kinds of generally significant developments with which world history is concerned. This principle of selection ac-

7. Kammen, p. 46.

cording to major developments is not as unfamiliar as it may appear. History teachers and texts already make such judgments when they teach, for example, the history of the United States rather than the histories of 50 individual states. Grouping together similar and related situations and developments, and then weighing their relative extent and import, can make the focus on *world* history a principle of selection and organization rather than a request to "cover" an impossible range of detail.

Moreover, the outcome statements listed in *Academic Preparation for College* focus on societies, cultures, and interactions that are of importance in the contemporary world. We are far from advocating a "presentist" approach that takes the world as it is found today and has no interest in how it came to be that way. Just the opposite. Many of the most important features of today's world have long and profound histories. As our earlier example indicated, high school students' understanding of current relations between India and Pakistan will go much further if it is built on some knowledge of the ancient contrast and competition between Hindu and Islamic cultures. At the same time, understanding the development of this cultural contrast is more important from the perspective of the contemporary world than the details of military and political strife on the Indian subcontinent in the twelfth and thirteenth centuries. By contrast, some of the major societies of the contemporary world—the Soviet Union and the United States—took political shape in relatively recent times, in the last three or four centuries. Indeed, this principle of selection often may lead curriculum to focus more on the study of cultural developments in earlier times and more on political, economic, and social developments in recent centuries.

One useful, if provocative, test of the power of such principles of selection is whether they lead to the exclusion of certain topics. By this test, the outcomes outlined in *Academic Preparation for College* direct attention away from two familiar history courses: those in Western (that is to say, European) history and those in ancient history, typically of the Mediterranean area. Such courses have many attractions; there are good reasons to include them as electives or preparation for the senior high school academic core we suggest here. However, such courses tend to ignore much of the rest of the world, and only some of the topics treated in them will bear the test of worldwide import and significance. Furthermore, the politics and economies discussed in them have less significance for the contemporary world than many other developments in the past.

There are, of course, many good ways to carry these principles of selection into courses and curriculum. One suggestion is to take the fundamental contrast between traditional and modern societies as a central chronological division. The study of world history could be separated into halves around the beginning of the seventeenth century, when the distinctive characteristics of the modern world began to emerge. Study of the earlier period would tend to focus on the geographical settings in which several major societies and cultures emerged, and on general similarities and contrasts in their major social, economic, political, and religious arrangements. Contacts between such societies would receive some attention, particularly when such contacts were vehicles for the spread of widely significant developments. Courses about this period could be arranged chronologically, with the selected major societies treated in parallel fashion, the course moving back and forth between contemporaneous developments. Another possibility is the world cultures or area studies approach in which the selected societies are treated successively. A richer treatment is possible if this part of the study of world history (that is, the pre-modern world) can be extended over several different years in the curriculum. But, in any event, not all societies can be treated. It is necessary to select among the seven or eight major possibilities. East Asian, South Asian, Mediterranean, and Western European societies seem important to include. If curriculum planning seeks to include connection with the course in United States history, then an additional choice of West African or Central American societies makes good sense.

Societies need to be understood on their own terms, not as appendages or future annexes to Western Europe; that is, they should not be viewed only from the eyes of outside observers. Moreover, earlier civilizations almost never coincided with current political boundaries; it is therefore less misleading to refer to them in geographical or cultural terms than in designations borrowed from present-day nation-states. Ending this half of the study of world history before the seventeenth century makes it easier for students to consider other societies in their own right, before their histories become so entangled with that of an expansive early modern Europe.

Treatment of world history since the seventeenth century can proceed according to a much more integrated chronology. Economic and political developments should receive greater stress, since the influence of those developments is still strongly felt. A fundamental theme could well be the spread of modernization. Since European countries were a powerful force in this process, the problem of treating other societies on their own terms will be especially troublesome. But modernization came to each society in a special way, conditioned by its previous cultural development. Indeed, how the traditional cultures of various societies interacted with the process of modernization can be a central focus of the study of world history.

Social Science

The courses in world and United States history should stand on their own and be treated as independent subjects within the social studies curriculum. In recent curriculum design historical study has sometimes been broken into fragments to be scattered through, or submerged within, a course of study primarily concerned with contemporary issues and social problems. One expert observer, for instance, recalls discovering that his daughter's high school history course consisted of study of one cultural group, one recent war, and two contemporary social problems.[8] It is difficult to identify the subject of such courses. Certainly they do not present history in any real sense of sequence and scope. True, the problem of "coverage" is reduced by selecting particular topics for attention, but at the cost of losing all sight of interrelated patterns of historical change. Moreover, the material about the past that is introduced in this manner probably will be understood as a reflection of present conditions rather than being explored on its own terms.

One argument advanced for courses of this kind is that they join history and the social sciences in common study. In truth, however,

---

8. Howard R. Lamar, "Encounter with a City: Education and the Promise of Local History." In *Teaching in America: The Common Ground* (New York: College Entrance Examination Board, 1985), p. 9.

they effectively disperse or dissolve any disciplinary approach so that none is available for study. We believe that history and the social sciences can and do assist one another within the curriculum, but this happens only as each is kept distinctive enough to clarify what one reveals of and for the other. The alliance works, so to speak, when the partners can still be seen as answering to one another rather than when all are assumed to share a single, vague character.

To consider how the alliance can work, remember, for example, that social science has its own "coverage" problems. *Academic Preparation for College* recommends that students become familiar with how to explore a social problem or institution by means of ideas drawn from several social sciences. This is difficult to achieve in a short space of study, and could involve textbook shortcuts that lead to superficial learning on the part of students. Social science concepts are as subject to rote learning as names and dates, and some texts present them as little more than labels with brief definitions to be memorized. But learning opportunities *are* deepened and increased if important concepts are introduced first through previous historical study. This is entirely appropriate, since social science concepts often provide important organizing questions for historical inquiry. The attention of social history to family history, for example, would not be possible without such concepts as "nuclear" and "extended" structures, socialization, and identity formation—all important ideas drawn from the social sciences.

Concepts studied in history courses can then be reintroduced and developed further in senior year social science study. This approach gives students time and recurring practice in absorbing conceptual ideas through the entire curriculum. But perhaps more importantly, it joins the use of such ideas with the study of substantive content. History in particular provides complex and detailed substance through which students begin to appreciate the power of concepts to organize large amounts of information and to raise significant questions. At the same time, it is precisely because historical information is both dense and various that some test of a concept's applicability and usefulness comes into play. This implicit "back and forth" between content and organizing idea prepares for learning in the senior year, when students should become familiar with the basic method of the social sciences—that is, the framing and testing of empirical hypotheses.

Of course, historical study does more than provide material for testing concepts. It also informs ensuing work in the social sciences by indicating how current experiences are products of historical change and continuity. Thus, inquiry into issues related to the contemporary family is helped when prior historical study leads students to question the assumption that traditional societies always treated the elderly with reverence or to see adolescence as a recent social phenomenon of industrial society involving delayed entrance into the world of work. Giving students the chance to make such connections requires, of course, that the social studies teachers in a school plan the scope of study in concert with one another, building course upon course, and identifying the ways in which the experiences of one relate to and increase the learning opportunities in all. Such coordination is important to all the suggestions in this book and basic to meeting the many demands of "coverage" encountered in the social studies curriculum.

III. The Outcomes and Developing Student Thought

In this chapter we approach the social studies curriculum and the design of courses within that curriculum from a special point of view. We want to suggest how curriculum deliberations can take into account the crucial matter of developing the way students think about human societies and their past.

In Chapter 1 it was argued that the emphasis in education needs to be shifted from what students do not know toward building on what they do know and are potentially able to do. Strengthening education for all students surely must start from this point. In Chapter 2 we indicated that many of the social studies outcome statements in *Academic Preparation for College* were intended to call attention to the emergence of important new bodies of knowledge, particularly in social history and in approaching the past from a global perspective. We also stressed in Chapter 2 the importance of developing a well-considered, coherent sequence among the courses that incorporate this new knowledge and held that an essential dimension in doing so was the development of student thought.

In this chapter we bring together these thoughts by illustrating how course material can be selected and organized so as not only to incorporate the bodies of knowledge outlined in Chapter 2 but also to provide for the exercise and development of students' understanding. Thus, this chapter provides an explication of the other social studies outcome statements described in *Academic Preparation for College*, those having to do with students' skills and understanding in history and the social sciences. It does so, however, in the context of actual knowledge as it might be presented in a social studies course and on the basis of the thought that students actually might bring with them into the classroom.

Planning a course of study must always involve a consideration of the prior experiences of students and their current knowledge and skills. Formal preparation is important, but we should not approach planning with narrow scholastic assumptions. The potential for learning that students bring to the classroom may be hidden not only from teachers, but also from themselves. As Alfred North Whitehead said, nobody "goes about with his knowledge clearly and consciously before him."[1] This caution is particularly important now when there is much talk of student deficiencies—when there seems to be a zeal in some quarters to insist on what students do not know or cannot do. Most teachers know, instead, that individual cases are seldom simple, and that particular students are not clear instances of "deficit" or achievement. Strengths and confusions can combine in the same student in ways that make it difficult to distinguish one from the other. Interests and development may follow a course that is not entirely open to demonstration in the classroom or through a test.

Moreover, it is important not to reduce learning to the narrow ability to recall factual information. This is particularly pertinent in historical studies where *what* students know and can do often has been estimated through their participation in a roll call of historical dates, events, and names. Such an estimate, Whitehead points out, likens the minds of students to facsimiles of textbooks. From this perspective, a successful student, when asked a question, simply looks into his or her mind to "select the right page to read aloud to the universe."[2]

This view suggests that students come to the classroom as blank pages, passively awaiting the imprint of textbook or lecture. We believe that education should not be approached from this presumption of lack, void, or inadequacy. Students already have begun to lead a life in history and many have begun to question their experiences in ways that, though small and personal, anticipate or involve historical thought. This may not be a matter of conscious awareness and almost certainly does not involve careful method, but it does suggest a prepared ground, a stirring. This argues against the presumption that students are barren of historical in-

---

1. Alfred North Whitehead, *The Aims of Education and Other Essays* (New York: New American Library, 1949), p. 37.
2. Ibid.

terest. It suggests a potentially more fruitful starting point from which to begin planning a social studies curriculum, one that does not move to fill in presumed blanks but relies instead on a confidence in the interests of students and their ability to think.

Recognizing Students' Historical Thought

The conviction that students bring important historical concerns with them to the social studies classroom deserves brief illustration. Autobiographical or retrospective accounts of youth often disclose more intense engagements with history than had been apparent or consciously known in the earlier time. We can take as an instance Ralph Ellison's personal essay entitled "Hidden Name and Complex Fate."[3] In this autobiographical statement Ellison reflects upon the life experiences that eventually entered into his analysis of American society in the novel *Invisible Man*. Looking back, he finds his later historical thought already emergent and prefigured in youthful questions and confusions. History, he suggests, had long since prepared in him the reason for its study.

Interestingly, Ellison sees these connections between an earlier and later time most revealed in an act of seeming reaction against, or rejection of, the past. This incident grew out of the difficulty he had felt from early childhood with his "troublesome middle name" and the link it suggested with Ralph Waldo Emerson. Why had his father chosen the name Ralph Waldo for him? What was the connection between himself, a black boy in Oklahoma, and "this remote Mr. Emerson" whose name he had been given? He felt that this identification with a far-removed time and person must intend something for his own present and future, but his attempts to figure this out only pointed to incongruities and deeper puzzlement. His father, who died when Ralph was three, was not there to provide an explanation; and the required reading of Emerson's essays in school brought no help. So Ellison recounts that at a certain moment in his teens he decided to suppress the difficult part of his name

---

3. Ralph Ellison, "Hidden Name and Complex Fate," in *Shadow and Act* (New York: New American Library, 1966).

and to search no more into its origins and possible meaning. "I reduced the 'Waldo' to a simple and, I hoped, mysterious 'W' and in my own reading I avoided Emerson's work like the plague."

Ellison conveys, however, that even in the midst of turning from the past he remained far more deeply involved with history than he could have fully known at the time. We can appreciate this stirring by relating it briefly to the outcomes statement in history presented in *Academic Preparation for College.*

- We see, for instance, that in the matter of the name young Ellison is anything but indifferent to history. Though we hear much about how students lack interest in the past, the glimpse we have here suggests a ferment of thought and feeling—an active effort, in fact, to achieve *understanding of the relationship between present and past.* Of course, we note impatience with things that remain "remote" and do not yield meaning, but what most impresses us, and Ellison himself, is not the momentarily stalled result, but rather the questioning spirit in the young boy who senses something is missed, not just for himself, but also of his father, if he fails to understand the connections across time and condition suggested by the name.

- In youth, this link with a distant time and place brings some bewilderment, but at the same time stretches young Ellison's mind and enlarges its potential reach. He does not think solely of his town and friends, or only of his own time, regardless of how much these seem to be the whole of the world. In thought, he attempts to embrace Emerson and faraway New England and include them in his sense of life. This forms the beginnings in him of a historical sense, complex in its emerging perceptions of *contrast* and *continuity* in the relationship between present and past. In youth, contrasts are most insistent and apparent in his thought. Young Ellison cannot grasp the identification with Emerson given differences of time, place, race, and social condition, but his father's choice of the name remains persistently "suggestive" of possible continuity. Even at a young age, Ellison senses that his father's affection for his son and admiration for Emerson have somehow drawn a line through time. Conditions may divide, but values point to an important unity.

- Moreover, young Ellison is acutely aware of the name as a possible *turning point* in time, as a sharp suggestive twist given to the course of his own life even before it had properly begun. In this, we note feelings of determinism, that things had been decided before one had any part in them. Yet, at the same time, Ellison knows that his father's choice might have been different and that the act of naming could have given his thought a very different direction. Why, young Ellison asks, "hadn't he named me after a hero, such as Jack Johnson, or a soldier like Colonel Charles Young, or a great seaman like Admiral Dewey, or an educator like Booker T. Washington, or a great orator and abolitionist like Frederick Douglass?" Ellison's thought, that is, is much absorbed in the event as it happened; but this includes a sense, as the historian Huizinga says, of how it "could have happened differently."[4] This "indeterminate point of view" toward given facts is a hallmark of historical inquiry and is an aspect of thought and feeling already prominent in Ellison's approach to the problem of his name.

- The part played by choice increases the stirring in Ellison to discover *cause and effect* explanations. What influences caused things to happen as they did rather than some other way? What in Emerson touched the life and mind of his father? What had his father brought to his reading (and his son hadn't) that created their different responses to the figure of Emerson? The instinct to seek cause and effect relations is more noticeable, at this point, in questions raised than in answers found. Still, we note Ellison's developing sense of his father as a figure in time, as one who looked behind and before, and who both acted and reacted in some historical sequence. Emerson was important to the puzzle, but perhaps more important was what his father made of Emerson and wanted of him for his son. Even in the midst of uncertainties, this appears to create in Ellison the sense of present and past as a two-way interaction in which neither side is all cause or all effect. In later life, this perception of how things

---

4. J. Huizinga, "Historical Conceptualization." In Fritz Stern (ed.), *The Varieties of History from Voltaire to the Present* (Cleveland, Ohio: World Publishing, 1956), p. 292.

mutually influence one another enlarges Ellison's scope of inquiry into the history of black people in this country and prompts him to look into the complex "reality of the American experience [both] as it shaped and was shaped by the lives of my own people."

■ As an adult, Ellison learned specific facts bearing on the puzzle of his name (including that his father had hoped he would become a poet); but the questions raised in his search now had expanded and, while still very personal, drew him to attempt a far-reaching *historical interpretation.* In orienting himself to the problem of his name, he ultimately recognized his participation in a long-standing interpretive inquiry among Americans (including the "remote" Emerson) which delved into "the puzzle of the one-and-the-many; the mystery of how each of us, despite his origins in diverse regions, with our diverse racial, cultural, religious backgrounds, speaking his own diverse idiom of the American in his own accent, is, nevertheless, American." Indeed, Ellison recognized that the question in his own name was related to the question in the name of the United States of America, with its suggestion of a land and people somehow unified by their diversity. From this perspective, answers for himself promised answers for the many. Viewed over time, the development of Ellison's youthful historical questioning and its contribution to his eventual historical awareness appear similar to Allan Nevins's description of the essence of historical thought:

> The most important part of history is really a series of problems. . . . The way to penetrate beneath the petty superficialities and come to grips with historical realities is to propound one incisive question after another, until the past ceases to look like a smooth record and becomes instead a rough and puzzling set of difficulties.[5]

The youthful stirrings described in Ellison's essay combine to involve him in questions of *how to approach the problem of change over time.* It is a large part of Ellison's intention to show how much such stirrings *are* present in youth, and to suggest their eventual

---

5. Allan Nevins, "The Gateway to History." In John A. Garraty (ed.), *Interpreting American History: Conversations with Historians, Part II* (New York: Macmillan, 1970), epigraph, p. v.

worth to learning, even though early on they remain unformed and partly hidden or make their appearance in acts of seeming rejection. The connections we discover with the learning outcomes described in *Academic Preparation for College* suggest the extent to which the historical skills we teach should be viewed as important refinements of native searchings, not as abstract principles of interest only to professional researchers. Such connections indicate that our students are not the historical amnesiacs they often are said to be, but rather are in the early beginnings of a still uncertain, often emotional, quest for personal and historical meaning.

Thus it would be a mistake to view the statements in *Academic Preparation for College* concerning historical skills as describing those skills only as they exist in an advanced state. To be sure, professional historians have developed these skills to a point of great sophistication. But to overlook their beginning in our students would be to miss much of what is in their minds and much of their potential for further development. It also would be to miss the important fact that all persons, as Carl Becker said, are in some fundamental sense their own historians.[6] Ellison's essay explores how personal thought about history can broaden and become more complex with experience. High school teachers seldom see the "end" of such a process of development or know the "hidden" questions that may eventually emerge. In the classroom, teachers deal in beginnings, introductions, in the early attempts students make to think historically along paths that are not strictly personal. They help students by asking them to achieve clear recognition of historical skills and by giving them some practice in their use. This approach to curricular planning and implementation builds on students' own powers of thought and prepares a clearer awareness of history as a distinctive way of learning and knowing.

Making Curricular Choices

Historical skills have little meaning for students, and perhaps less acceptance, if taught abstractly. They are recognized and used

---

6. Carl Becker, *Everyman His Own Historian* (Chicago: Quadrangle Books, 1966).

more readily when introduced in conjunction with, and as central to, inquiry into substantive historical topics, themes, or questions. Consequently, we shall now illustrate how the specific skills listed in *Academic Preparation for College* might be included in the substantive study of United States history. For purposes of discussion, we can continue with Ellison's focus on the issue of the "one-and-the-many" and consider it through the topic of the migration of peoples, voluntary or forced, which forms such an important part of the United States historical basis.

This, of course, is only one of many topics from which a framework of study might be built. Industrialization, say, could work equally well. The point is not to prescribe a content, but to emphasize that skills become meaningful only through engagement with content. Therefore, before turning to the specific skills, it is useful to consider—as in the case of every such choice—how the topic incorporates the major subject matter considerations discussed in Chapter 2.

▪ Migration is a recurring feature in United States history. Although it is not subject to conventional periodization, it reappears as a major feature of the American experience from the first settlements through the mobility of the changing population—including, for example, westward expansion and the movement from farms to cities—to the recent waves of immigration from Latin America and Asia. This importance over time leads historians Dinnerstein and Jaher to conclude that "America was created and shaped by successive waves of immigrants."[7] Perhaps this statement needs some qualification, but the continuing significance of migration in the making of American life is undeniable and provides a variety of opportunities to take up the study of change over time. This permits easy adjustment of the topic to most chronological frameworks and, more importantly, provides opportunities to consider the interrelatedness of migration with other key topics (for example, urbanization, industrialization, and population growth) either over time or at critical historical junctures.

---

7. Leonard Dinnerstein and Frederic Cople Jaher (eds.), *The Aliens: A History of Ethnic Minorities in America* (New York: Appleton-Century-Crofts, 1970), p. 3.

- Migration has a major place in the way that Americans think about themselves. As one foreign observer puts it, the emphasis we place on this topic is "scarcely surprising in view of the intimate connection which exists between migration and the American experience. . . . The influx of diverse European, African, and Asiatic strains [induces] a self-consciousness about ethnic origins, the juxtaposition of minorities and concern for the effect of ethnic mixture upon the national character and institutions which is unique in modern history."[8] Study of migration, therefore, offers perspective on, and understanding of, important social concerns and provides opportunities to present historical study as fundamental to ongoing thought about our national life instead of as memorization of facts.

- Migration is an important topic in social history's enterprise of studying the activities of ordinary people. Indeed, the interests of current scholarship were informed in important ways by ground-breaking studies of how the historical process of migration impacted upon family structure and life in immigrant populations. Moreover, migration is part of the historical background, or immediate past, of most Americans. Its study looks into a drama that has somehow touched the life of a majority of citizens and explores what is at once a diverse experience and a common heritage.

- Inquiry into migration encourages global reach and perspective. In its study, we inquire not only into the arrival of peoples and how they settled or moved about, but also where they came from and what kind of lives they led before their departure. More and more, we also look into why many returned to the land of origin. This large vision is appropriate to a pluralistic society like our own, and study also can be varied in its specific reference depending on students' backgrounds, the high school's geographical location, the teacher's preparation, and the available materials. Moverover, thinking of migration to the United States as coming

---

8. Frank Thistlethwaite, "Migration from Europe Overseas in the Nineteenth and Twentieth Centuries." In Stanley N. Katz and Stanley I. Kutler (eds.), *New Perspectives on the American Past*, vol. 2, *1877 to the Present* (Boston: Little, Brown, 1969), p. 53.

from other societies with their own distinctive features and ways of life provides a useful principle for organizing an immediately preceding world history course. Although it would be a distortion to organize the study of world history on the basis of what has been "contributed" to the United States, many choices can be made that will build both factual and conceptual bridges to the study of United States history. It also is possible to compare the United States as a society experiencing migration with other cases such as the Middle East at present or India at earlier points in history.

■ Inquiry into migration also encourages a close connection between historical study and the understanding of social science concepts and methods. It is, for example, a historical point of importance that American social science formed many of its critical issues through the study of social questions created by large-scale immigration to this country in the late nineteenth and early twentieth centuries. And, as Sigmund Diamond has pointed out, migration and relocation of groups of people have always prompted questions about how society functions and have proven "an extraordinary stimulus to social thought in general."[9] Thus, study of migration in a United States history course will provide many opportunities for student practice in the use of social science concepts, building close curricular connections with ensuing social science courses. It has direct bearing on American political behavior, of course, but the ideas employed in the study of migration also can be developed further in the study of anthropology, economics, and psychology as well as in sociology and political science.

Linking Historical Skills and Content

With this indication of how a focus on migration in a United States history course might fit with curricular considerations developed in

---

9. Sigmund Diamond, "The European Basis of American Civilization." In John A. Garraty (ed.), *Interpreting American History: Conversations with Historians, Part I* (New York: Macmillan, 1970), p. 7.

Chapter 2, we turn to illustrating how taking up an expanded version of Ellison's problem of the "one-and-the-many" can support development of the historical skills we saw presaged in Ellison's youth. A well-conceived high school history course will provide many opportunities that help students recognize these skills and apply them in an introductory, but explicit, way in their thought.

- *Some understanding of the relationship between present and past, including contrasts between contemporary institutions and values and those of the past, the reasons for these contrasts, and leading continuities between past and present.*

Questions of sociohistorical change are central to any inquiry into migration. For example, a past and present usually meet, and sometimes collide, when immigrants enter a receiving country. Often the movement of peoples from a foreign land to the United States involves passage from a more traditional to a more modern society, thus absorbing all concerned to some extent in the historical change of what has been called "the great transformation." Students, then, can apply knowledge of major differences between traditional and modern social structures (for example, community, family, and economy) learned in the previous world history course to study of the experience of migrant groups.

Moreover, students should acquire an understanding of the conceptual framework through which historians attempt to grasp the nature and degree of change in immigrant groups created by interaction with, and adjustment to, the receiving society. Important concepts include acculturation (acquisition of the receiving society's traits, such as language), assimilation (social integration, as through intermarriage), and pluralism (retention of old traits and behavior patterns). Students also should begin to recognize the potential importance of such features as religion, race, class, and gender in influencing rate or degree of change.

Such considerations help focus questions about the impact of new conditions on immigrant groups. Historians know, however, that change is a two-way process and that immigration has played a part in shaping and developing American life. This is a difficult matter to assess, but it should not be dismissed by simple reference to distinguished individuals of foreign birth. Students can come to understand that the flow of immigration has contributed significantly to other major trends in United States history (for example, industrialization, urbanization) and that the course of national development would have been much different without it. For example, students should know that immigration provided much of the labor force for American industrial expansion in the nineteenth and early twentieth centuries, including the building of the national systems of transportation and communication. They should be able to explore the social and economic significance of such facts as that by 1900, the majority of employees in each of the leading American industries was of immigrant origin. Moreover, they should know that the contribution is not of numbers alone, but that basic industries—textiles, mining, and iron and steel—leaned heavily on immigrant skill and expertise for their technical development.

▪ *The ability to identify major historical turning points.*

Study of migration affords students many opportunities to identify and characterize historical turning points. For example, they can note different periods of migration and ask how one may be distinguished from another. The wave of so-called "new immigration" to this country in the late nineteenth and early twentieth centuries provides one possible focus for analysis. Students might not only note a shift in area of origin from previous migrations (from the north and west of Europe to southern and central regions), but also take into account differences in other major characteristics of the migrating groups such as religion, language, ethnicity, race, and class. These characteristics can in turn be applied comparatively to other migrations such as the recent flow of migrants from Asia and Latin America or to the internal migration of blacks from the rural South to the urban North in the early twentieth century.

The important point is to help students achieve a conceptual grasp of turning points, and not just regard change as a reference to names, dates, and incidents. The Haymarket Riot of 1886 was an important event in social and political history, but it cannot be grasped as such without an understanding of major currents of change that gave it its special character. Students then can apply conceptual knowledge to related questions in the overall chronological framework. Why, for example, do we discover different patterns of reception for different waves of immigration—and for different migrant groups—by the dominant American society? And how does this shed light on the practice of democratic values in this country? Such questions deepen and enliven study of the political chronology by asking how trends in immigration affected the theory and practice of American democracy. As one historian has said, when the Founding Fathers proclaimed the idea of equality they could not have envisaged that the republic would be sought out by persons "from every corner of the earth anxious to test the truth of what they proclaimed."[10]

■ *The ability to recognize historical cause and effect.*

Identification of historical turning points in migration leads naturally to questions about cause and effect. What started a period of migration and what kept it going? Students can come to recognize that this question must be asked in at least two ways. One can say that immigrants came to the United States or that they left their land of origin. Were they "pulled" by inducements of the new place or "pushed" by difficulties and discouragements in the old? Migration is a movement both away and toward, and speculation about the importance of each side of the impulse begins to take students into the complexity of historical causation.

The recognition of complexity is increased as students consider the weight to be given to each side. For example, in the period of "new immigration" mentioned above, such factors as agricultural dislocation and social confinement in the place of origin must be combined with employment opportunities and anticipated freedom in the urban United States to explain the migrant flow. As students consider these factors, they once again have the opportunity to recognize that migration is not an isolated phenomenon, but is interrelated with other large historical processes such as industrialization and urbanization. For example, students should be aware that new conditions of industrial labor and urban living were alien to the previous experience of *both* native and foreign-born and, therefore, that change must be viewed in part as "*mutual* transformations of immigrants and other Americans in the face of industrial

---

10. Maldwyn Allen Jones, "The Impact of Immigration." In Trevor Colbourn and James T. Patterson (eds.), *The American Past in Perspective*, vol. 2, *Since 1865* (Boston: Allyn and Bacon, 1970), p. 67.

upheaval."[11] From this perspective, tensions that emerged between groups appear less a matter of ethnic divisions than the result of distress experienced by the total population in adapting to a new historical environment.

Cause and effect considerations also open the way for further comparative analysis of migrations. Students, for instance, can ask how the migration of blacks from the rural South to the urban North during the early decades of the twentieth century is like or unlike the "new immigration." Both evidence the importance in migration of rural poverty and agricultural disruption at the point of origin with employment opportunities made possible by industrial expansion in the intended destination. But in the case of the black migration we are aware of the part played by the curtailment of political and civil rights. This raises the question of to what extent most migrations, or important aspects of them, should be considered as acts of social and political protest. Here once again we see a link between the topic of migration and political frameworks. Understanding socioeconomic factors should not disregard the part played by the "spirit of revolt" in the movement of peoples.[12]

- *Some ability to develop historical interpretations.*

In-depth study of a topic such as migration develops better appreciation of how, as Carl Becker said, "it is impossible to divorce history from life."[13] The questions of historians do not derive from antiquarian impulses. They are woven from the things of our existence and direct themselves to the need to know where we have been so we can understand where we are and to anticipate where we want to go.

But, practice in historical skills also can help students see that the very centrality of a question to our own interests can lead to undue emphasis or partial explanation. For instance, the impor-

---

11. Julie Leininger Pycior. "Acculturation and Pluralism in Recent Studies of American Immigration History." In *Ethnic and Immigration Groups: The United States, Canada, and England,* Institute for Research in History (New York: Haworth, 1983), p. 25.

12. Thistlethwaite, p. 79.

13. Becker, p. 242.

tance of migration in our national history can lead Americans, one observer says, to focus on "the consequences and not the causes of migration . . . and, moreover, the consequences in the receiving, not the sending country."[14] Attention to questions of cause and effect—the "push" and "pull" factors discussed above—requires students to enlarge their vision and see why historians now feel the need to correct this imbalance if we are to have more satisfactory interpretations. Students can be aware of migration as not only an event in this country but also as an event in Ireland or in the Philippines. And they also can see, therefore, that questions such as the one of "immigrant adjustment" cannot be asked only with reference to conditions in this country, but as a review of recent scholarship suggests, we also need increased knowledge of "the mother culture" in order to assess "the degree of cultural change in the adopted land."[15]

We do not suggest, of course, that students should arrive at complete answers to all or most questions about migration, but we do believe they should have experience in how historical inquiry proceeds through development of new or revised interpretive approaches. In this case, a more global perspective on a historical phenomenon raises fresh questions and builds a more complete structure of inquiry. Students can learn that immigration is more than the familiar story of the "peopling" of the United States and become aware of why historians are drawn, as Thistlethwaite suggests, to look at it as a total process and ask into the "complete sequences of experiences" from the "first intimations of dislodgement at home to ultimate reconciliation or defeat abroad."[16] Students can come to grasp, then, that the development of a historical interpretation may not only include new answers but also suggest a different framework for asking questions.

In this regard, students can begin to understand how quantitative data open new lines of inquiry. We know, for example, that approximately 33 million immigrants arrived in the United States between 1821 and 1924. This information begins to acquaint stu-

---

14. Thistlethwaite, p. 55.

15. Pycior, p. 30.

16. Thistlethwaite, p. 56.

dents with the order of magnitude of the phenomenon. They also can learn, however, that approximately 55 million people emigrated from Europe during the same period. This points to the importance of the United States in the migration of European peoples (drawing more than three-fifths of the total number), but also indicates once again that the movement to this country was only one part of a large phenomenon. Where did the others go and what drew them? Numbers for the same period suggest the need for a hemispheric perspective on the question. Estimates indicate that Argentina received 5.4 million immigrants; Brazil, 3.8 million; and Canada, 4.5 million. Here students should be able to grasp the important difference between absolute numbers of immigrants and rate of immigration into a country. If, for instance, students relate the numbers above to estimates of the intensity of immigration (the number of immigrants in proportion to population), they should begin to construct a more meaningful frame of reference for thinking about the impact of immigration on receiving countries. In the decade 1901-1910, for example, figures on the intensity of immigration in rates per hundred thousand were: United States just over 1,000, Canada 1,500, Argentina 3,000.

Thus students, like ourselves, begin to see that Ellison's question of the "one-and-the-many" is not one for Americans alone. To be sure, the matter was special for a black youth in Oklahoma (or for the adult writer in New York City), but that it must have been in some way at the heart of historical experience for so many others around the globe makes the problem of its uniqueness at once less obvious and all the more compelling. By planning a curriculum around such questions teachers can not only raise important historical issues but also involve students in learning that develops increasingly sophisticated historical skills.

IV. Teaching History and Social Sciences

The most commonplace instructional material in any social studies classroom is the textbook. Used effectively, it can serve a number of important functions. It provides a basis both for coverage of important subject matter and common study materials for students. Most texts also suggest additional readings, raise questions about the materials studied, and are useful as references as well as for summary and review. Textbooks also include such important features as maps, graphs, tables, and photographs that are helpful for skills development.[1]

Used imaginatively, textbooks also can assist in the development of student thought. That history texts, for example, provide coverage of a long sweep of time presents opportunities for students to recognize the *problem of change over time*. If strictly followed section by section, texts often offer a thin, sometimes tedious, recounting of the past; but teachers are not bound to conduct study according to this scheme of organization. They can, for example, ask students to step back from the narrative flow and contrast the text's descriptions of key institutions at different points in time. This activity might focus on descriptions of the function of the state in the seventeenth and nineteenth centuries or the differences between "extended" and "nuclear" family structure in traditional and modern society. In this way, students become more sharply aware of change and also better acquainted with its essential features.

Despite their advantages and possibilities, textbooks should not dominate in school study to the extent they often do. Some estimates suggest that they make up as much as 90 percent of the

---

1. Hazel W. Hertzberg, "Students, Methods and Materials of Instruction." In Matthew T. Downey (ed.), *History in the Schools* (Washington, D.C.: National Council for the Social Studies, 1985), pp. 25-39.

course of study in many school situations. This is too much, given the limitations of the textbook form. The presentation of the past they make cannot entirely, or enough, escape conveying the idea of a static body of familiar knowledge transmitted through standard views. In consequence, a fundamental teaching issue concerns how to make certain that students see, in Frederick Jackson Turner's words, "that history is not shut up in a book."[2] Teachers must help students know that history involves *"all the remains that have come down to us from the past, studied with all the critical and interpretive power that the present can bring to the task."*[3]

An important approach to this problem continues to be introducing students to, and having them work with, relevant source materials and "survivals" from the past. This can free students from the confines of the textbook and place them in more direct relation to a particular past. Conducted effectively, this kind of study helps students gain a more vivid sense of the past, develop critical skills needed in dealing with historical information, and achieve a better understanding of historical inquiry and the development of historical interpretations. Once students have experience in working with actual survivals from the past, they begin to see that history is less a familiar series of names and incidents to be memorized than a challenge to critical thought, less standard answers than a number of significant questions open to diverse treatment and interpretation.

But this approach is not without problems. First, there is the challenge of abundance. How does one select from all that history offers? The materials, Turner points out, include

> . . . all that remains from the ages gone by—in papers, roads, mounds, customs, languages; in monuments, coins, medals, names, titles, inscriptions, charters; in contemporary annals and chronicles; . . . Wherever there remains a chipped flint, a spearhead, a piece of pottery, a pyramid, a picture, a poem, a coliseum, or a coin, there is history."[4]

---

2. Frederick Jackson Turner, "An American Definition of History." In Fritz Stern (ed.), *The Varieties of History from Voltaire to the Present* (Cleveland, Ohio: World Publishing, 1956), p. 201.

3. Ibid.

4. Ibid., pp. 201-202.

This list could be easily expanded—photographs, films, cartoons, songs, ledgers, charts, graphs, tables. The variety and amount of material is enormous, and close attention to even a single source can demand a great deal of attention from both teachers and students in conditions where classroom time is very limited.

This challenge has met with several responses. At one extreme, some have advocated discarding textbooks almost completely and basing high school history on "source" study. In the 1960s, for example, one approach proceeded on the assumption that students should be taught to "think like" professional historians and to practice the historical method, just as at the same time students of science were being asked to "think like" scientists and to practice the scientific method. This usually involved focusing the whole of a study on one or two historical events (for example, the Salem witch trials), immersing students in large quantities of relevant primary sources, and then asking them to conduct a historical investigation along lines of professional method.

The problems with this approach in practice were many: first, few students began with enough history, enough context, to "think like" professional historians with anything like the sophistication demanded by the task; second, the study was so narrowly focused, and involved such attention to fragments of data, that students never acquired the historical perspective and general body of knowledge that they lacked in the beginning; third, the total activity presupposed the completion of a historical analysis appropriate perhaps to graduate students, but not to high school students just beginning critical thought and interpretation.

The shortcomings of this experience should not, however, lead teachers to doubt the gains that can come to students through appropriate study of historical sources. Nor should pressures of time lead to token inclusion of bits of historical material. This makes source material appear marginal to the total scope of study and provides only a fragmentary learning experience. The key is to select material that both builds upon and supplements other reading in the organizing framework of study and that, within a relatively short period of study, gives students a coherent experience in historical thought and interpretation. We will illustrate this approach through a discussion of how teachers used a school musical production to enrich study in a world history course, particularly to promote learning in the use of a major concept.

The King and I

The concept of modernization can be very useful to high school students of history and the social sciences. *Academic Preparation for College* emphasizes that "we live in a distinct kind of society and all people need to understand how such modern societies function and how they have developed." The concept can help students organize the enormous variety of the human past. C. E. Black has suggested that modernization during the last three or four centuries represents a revolutionary transformation in human affairs comparable in scope and intensity only to the emergence of the major civilizations thousands of years ago, or to the emergence of human beings themselves many, many millennia before that.[5]

Not only does modernization represent a turning point of long-range and global significance, the concept also can help students understand the interaction of the various aspects of history. It places the central focus on social history, on how groups of people have lived together in different times and places, and on how, in modern times, those places are increasingly and predominantly cities. But modernization is a process arising from scientific and technological knowledge and involving a shift to industrial economies from primarily agricultural ones. It involves new conceptions of the sovereign state and autonomous individuals. Thus, not only social arrangements but also intellectual, economic, political, and psychological considerations can be brought together when history students begin to employ and elaborate an understanding of modernization. Because that understanding involves many concepts fundamental to the various social sciences—indeed, to a significant extent, the social sciences are a distinctly modern form of knowledge—working with the concept of modernization can prepare stu-

---

5. C. E. Black, *The Dynamics of Modernization: A Study in Comparative History* (New York: Harper & Row, 1967), pp. 1-5.

dents for later study of one or more of the social sciences. Finally, of course, modernization continues to be a major trend in today's world. Beginning to understand it, and reactions to it, will introduce students to an important part of the context of contemporary diplomacy and economics.

The very scope and power of the concept of modernization, however, can create difficulties for high school students. The abstract terms and sweeping generalizations with which a textbook might develop the concept are not how students—or, for that matter, historians—typically apprehend the past. The problem for teachers is to provide a means by which the general can be seen in the particular, the abstract in the specific. Moreover, the point of acquiring the concept is not that students should be able to recite an inventory of associated features or even to characterize a particular historical case as an instance of those features. The concept is useful when students can begin to employ its power, organizing, relating, and explaining diverse phenomena in ways that lead to further questions, observations, and interpretations. Consequently, high school history teachers might well wish to supplement textbook references to modernization with a simple working model of the concept, one familiar to their students and one susceptible to further tinkering.

In a particular high school some teachers thought that they had found such a working model when the theater teacher chose for the spring production that staple of high school musicals, Rodgers and Hammerstein's *The King and I*.[6] Attracted by the possibility of interdisciplinary cooperation, these history teachers began to consider what could be made of the opportunity, in spite of the obvious limitations of the play as a vehicle for historical understanding. The limitations are not inconsiderable. *The King and I* is a 1951 Broadway musical based most immediately on a 1946 Hollywood movie. Both sprang from a 1943 bestseller, which author Margaret Landon based rather loosely on the 1870 and 1872 books by Anna Leonowens. Since Mrs. Leonowens was herself a foreigner

---

6. Richard Rodgers and Oscar Hammerstein II, "The King and I," in *6 Plays by Rodgers and Hammerstein* (New York: Random House, 1959).

in the Siam of the 1860s, *The King and I* is many times removed from what historians regard as primary source material.

Moreover, Rodgers and Hammerstein hardly had been concerned with historically authentic reconstruction. Four days before the show opened on Broadway, Richard Rodgers explained in the *New York Herald Tribune* that "if one were to reproduce with accuracy" the Siam of the mid-nineteenth century, "it seems probable you would end repelling completely the Western eye, ear, nose and sense of touch."[7] This view extended to the music and language of the play. "Our people want to feel as deeply as possible, and they cannot be made to do so with music they do not understand, anymore than they can be made to react emotionally to a foreign tongue." Oscar Hammerstein had considered using the Thai language for the show but, after hearing it spoken, ended up writing instructions that "throughout the play, the Siamese language will be represented by certain sounds made in the orchestra. Siamese words will never be literally pronounced." One result was that—as the *New Yorker* observed at the time of the original Broadway production—"all but half a dozen members of the cast speak the sort of pidgin English that is used on stage and screen for the presentation of every kind of foreigner from Kurd to Eskimo, and that calls blindly for the elimination of 'the' ('to whom I pay vast sum of twenty pounds a year') and of the introductory 'it' ('Is a puzzlement')."[8]

Finally, any attempt to use *The King and I* as a working model to exercise historical understanding will encounter the fact that an implied romantic attraction between Anna and the King of Siam and an explicit romance between Tuptim, a slave, and Lun Tha, the emissary who brought her from Burma, have been imposed on the historical material. The placement of songs in the show emphasizes these elements, and the need for Rodgers and Hammerstein to work "within our own romantic medium" further challenges any effort to get at and work with the genuine historical content that shows through in *The King and I*.

---

7. Richard Rodgers, "The Background Is Siam, The Music Pure Broadway," *The New York Herald Tribune*, October 25, 1951.

8. John Lardner, "The Surefire Boys in Siam," *New Yorker*, April 7, 1951.

Against these limitations a history teacher in this particular high school could weigh several other factors. Most persuasive would be that students already are familiar with the musical and in worrying about how to present it and about why the various characters do what they do, the students have begun to move about within the framework of the show, making it their own. Teachers know that student interest and involvement signal greater possibilities. Further, at the other end of the long bridge that teachers might help students build lies the historical fact that Anna Leonowens actually did live and work in mid-nineteenth-century Siam, just when the first modern nations, Britain and France, swirled about and threatened that country. Moreover, it is a particularly interesting situation since Siam, like Russia, China, and Japan, moved into modernization without being either settled by Western Europeans or conquered by them. And, in some sense, modernization does seem to be the pivot of the play. In what is perhaps the central confrontation of the play (Act I, Scene 4) Anna reproves the king in the terms of his own contradictory feelings about his country: "A land where there is talk of honor, and a wish for Siam to take her place among the modern nations of the world! Where there is talk of great changes, but where everything still remains according to the wishes of the King!"

The long chain of events that leads from Southeast Asia in the nineteenth century to an amateur production in a high school auditorium could well be as far beyond the reach of typical high school students as the manipulation and application of such abstractions as modernization, sovereignty, and identity. A teacher, however, might approach the play inductively, very much as a historian might approach analysis of a primary source document.

A teacher's first step might be to insert the action of the story into a historical context. Ask students, using only their copy of the play, a dictionary, and the maps in their world history textbook, to figure out where and when the play is supposed to have occurred. The question about the supposed location of the play can be answered mechanically, but that answer may prompt some fertile questions. Using a dictionary will help students unravel the fact that what the play calls Siam is what their maps of the contemporary world refer to as Thailand. This will help students locate some other place references in the play—Singapore, Burma, China, and so on—but also will raise some interesting questions. Why was Siam renamed? Have other countries been renamed? Why? What does Thailand mean, anyway? Such questions provide leads to which the teacher may want to return after the lesson has developed further.

Reading Act I will supply the information that the play is set during the presidency of Abraham Lincoln, perhaps soon after the Emancipation Proclamation. The king, even before writing to Lincoln, identifies himself unhesitatingly as someone who is against slavery. This way of locating the supposed time of the play has several advantages over the teacher's simply supplying the date 1863 or 1864. Not only does it exercise students' analytic and inferential skills, but also it begins to build a temporal context by reference to events that students are likely already to find familiar. Not incidentally, that context displays the history of the United States in a global perspective, rather than giving the usual impression of its being sealed off from any outside connections. As many teachers of 14- and 15-year-old students will recognize, however, there is likely to be another conversation going on at this point. The back rows will be buzzing with imaginative variations on the offer in the king's letter to send elephants to President Lincoln. The thought of the huge beasts lumbering into battle during the American Civil War is funny, and it is worth joining in on the laughter. Why elephants are funny is a question that discloses not only a central assumption of the play, but also a central reality of nineteenth-century imperialism.

Having located the play in a real time and place, the teacher may well want to ask what Anna, this very British lady, is doing in Siam, anyway. She is a kind of reverse immigrant, going from a modern to a traditional society. The answer will come back straight out of the play: she has come to run a school for the king. This answer leads on toward two other sets of questions. One set has to do with "push" factors, the other with the "pull" of Siam. Why is Anna going to run a school in Siam? Answers such as, "She was in Singapore" and "Her husband died" lead to a further question about what Anna and her husband might have been doing in Singapore. That question might point back to discussions in the textbook of British imperialism.

That Anna was coming to Siam to run a school for the king also can lead to an even more interesting set of questions, triggered by the query, "Why would the king of Siam want an English school?" Students may come up with many imaginative answers, but here it would be worth holding them close to the evidence they have read in the text. There they would find the king's own answer, given directly to Anna: "You are part of a general plan I have for bringing to Siam what is good in Western culture. Already I have brought a printing press here for printing." What else is good about Western culture? The king promptly provides an answer by bestowing a high compliment on Anna for already having looked into his plan for Siam: "Ha! This is scientific." Moments later Lady Thiang, the king's head wife, confirms the value Siam finds in the school-teacher: "Because you scientific. Not lowly, like woman." This line will doubtless bring another round of buzzing to most classrooms and teachers may not have the opportunity to pursue the challenging question of what printing presses and science have to do with each other. In any case, the essential point will have been established: the king has brought Anna to Siam because he respects Western science. Already these high school students will have some relevant observations to make about the common interpretation that modern culture was simply imposed or bestowed upon the non-Western world.

With *The King and I* located in a definite place and time, and with the play set in motion by the king's desire to import Western scientific learning, history teachers might find it useful to direct attention promptly to the central conflicts of the play. Although these tensions may seem trivial from a dramatic point of view, they display rather sharply some contrasting features of modern and traditional societies. In doing so it will be necessary to help students sidestep the patina of romance that has been imposed on the central characters and also to encourage students to take seriously the viewpoints of both characters, to assume that both have grounds for their positions. In doing the latter it will be helpful if some of the students are involved in the school's production of the play, with at least a few "getting into" the characters of the king and those around him. Understanding the king's position will come less easily to most students than sharing Anna's assumptions.

Students quickly will discover that a primary source of conflict in Act I is that Anna wants to live in a home outside the palace, a desire the king and his ministers do not understand and staunchly resist: "You teach in palace, you shall live in palace." Anna's contrary assertions likewise refer to the workplace: ". . . I will *teach* in the palace, but I must have a house of my own—where I can go at the end of the day when my duties are over." Anna's insistence on the separation of work from other parts of life already had been emphasized when the delegation receiving her into Siam began immediately to inquire about her friends, her deceased husband, and so on. What may have been courtesy on one side was perceived as rudeness on the other. "Tell your master his business with me is in my capacity of schoolteacher to the royal children. He has no right to pry into my personal affairs." Teachers' questions can help students understand both sides of this conflict over the distinctively modern segregation of work and private life by pointing toward its relation to the modern, industrial organization of work. "Well, what kind of job would make people work outside their homes? Do farmers have to leave home to go to work?"

Students will be quick to point out that the king had agreed to give Anna a house of her own and Anna herself makes a great deal of the contractual nature of her relationship to the king. "I came here to work. I must support myself and my young son. And I shall take nothing less than what I have been promised. . . . I have made a bargain, and I shall live up to my part of it. But I expect a bargain to be kept on both sides." Students probably will have a hard time appreciating the king's side of this conflict, but there will be no mistaking the airy nonchalance with which he regards the contractual view of employment. He simply does not remember the words of his letter. When challenged, he thunders: "I will do remembering. Who is King? . . . I do not know of any promises. I do not know anything but that you are my servant." This moment is one of the sharpest conflicts in the play and soon gives rise to a seething soliloquy in which Anna contrasts the two views of work relations:

> Your servant! Your servant!
> Indeed I'm not your servant
> (Although you give me less than servant's pay)
> I'm a free and independent employé . . . employee.

Since students might find it difficult to understand how anyone could work in any other way than as an independent and paid employee, it is worth pointing out that Anna herself is not immune to feeling other sorts of work obligations. Later in the play the king gives Anna a valuable ring. Anna confesses to the Kralahome, the king's chief minister, that this places her in "a rather embarrassing position." She goes on to say that "I was intending to ask him for a rise in salary. And now . . ." The Kralahome finishes her thought: "And now it will be difficult to ask." At this point a teacher might provoke a very lively discussion by asking if students believe they should be paid for work they do at home. All sorts of alarming responses are possible, but some students will probably offer the conventional "right" answer that working at home and working outside are "different." Most teachers will have to restrain themselves to keep from pronouncing too mightily on this reappearance of the modern distinction between the home and the workplace. Nonetheless, that students find themselves using the same distinction that we attribute to the nineteenth century can be helpful. It may even be possible to provoke some further understanding of the contrasting social arrangements that preceded modern societies by asking students a hypothetical question: "What if working at home and working at a job weren't so different?"

The capacity of high school students for such sustained exegesis of a text is generally fairly limited. Consequently, as Anna and the king compromise their differences to deal with a common threat toward the end of Act I, a teacher may want to shift approaches and begin to draw discussion of *The King and I* back toward the historical narrative that might be found in the textbook or other sources. This shift would be timely, since Act II treats the great issues of maintaining national sovereignty and overcoming slavery almost exclusively as comedy and romantic melodrama, respectively.

Noting that the play refers only to the coming of an English gunboat, a teacher might ask students to discover if the king's— and Anna's—fears for Siam are realistic. Some students might be asked to review their textbooks and report on what had been going on in India about the supposed time of the play. Another group might be asked to report on events in China. Learning about such events as the Opium Wars—which were very much in the mind of the historical King Mongkut—will help students understand that maintaining the sovereignty of Siam was no small accomplishment.

Noting that in the play Anna and the king combined forces on this matter, a teacher might ask if national independence is a modern or a traditional value. Reading further into the twentieth-century histories of India and China will help answer this question, of course, and the question itself will help check an inevitable tendency to see the king and Anna as representing traditional and modern societies, respectively. This is good history and good drama. Early in the discussion of the play the king was understood as seeking to import modern science, and seeing such characters as entertaining conflicting impulses is both true to life and good literature. That is why the king's offer of elephants to Abraham Lincoln was both funny and possible. At other moments the king knew—as audiences know—that elephants were no match for the industrial power that lay behind English gunboats. In historical fact Abraham Lincoln answered King Mongkut's letter by noting that Americans had found steampower, both on land and water, quite satisfactory.

The other great issue of Act II of *The King and I* concerns slavery, but history teachers will find its treatment there so mixed up with the obligatory romance in this kind of play that it will be difficult to make anything of the matter directly. They might instead follow the clue provided by the dance scene in which the plight of Tuptim, the slave girl, is expressed through the story of Eliza in Harriet Beecher Stowe's novel concerning slavery in the United States, *Uncle Tom's Cabin*. Again teachers might turn their students' attention to the wider world of the nineteenth century by asking how widespread slavery, and opposition to it, was. Students' reports might deal not only with the United States but perhaps most notably with the 1861 Emancipation Decree in Russia. From this global perspective, students may come to see Anna's insistence on being a "free and independent employee" as a fundamentally important aspect of modernization. They also will have an opportunity to discover that there were different kinds of unfree labor and various routes by which societies moved away from it.

Many other aspects of modernization might be approached through *The King and I*, among them changing views of religion and the status of women. But a teacher will not want to leave the play without working a bit with its ending, for in many ways the death of the king was Hammerstein's most effective invention. That the king dies of a broken heart, shamed because he is unable personally to punish Tuptim for her attempted escape, will leave students—as it must—both unsympathetic and skeptical. They will be unsympathetic—indeed actively hostile—because they recognize in every individual an innate dignity that slavery denied. This can be a valuable teaching moment. Ultimately students of history must encounter the "otherness" of much of the past, must recognize that things were not always as we would wish or imagine them to be. It is just this "otherness" that Rodgers and Hammerstein largely omitted from their play for fear that it would repel their audiences. In the broken heart scene, of course, part of the king, finally the dominant part, does draw back from perpetrating the horrors of slavery—as in historical fact his son actually did.

To help students appreciate the internal conflict the king feels in this scene, ask them to consider his reaction when Anna discusses the women who are his many wives. "We do not look on women as just human females. They are . . . Well, take yourself. You are not just a human male." The king's response does not refer to any intrinsic personal quality but to his role, his status in society: "I am King." The play provides many indications as to what it means to be king. Throughout the play the king is referred to by title, not name. The king cannot take advice. The king must be certain as his father was before him. The king is bound by duty. "But no matter what I think, I must go on living life. As leader of my kingdom, I must *go* forth. . . ." Just before the king finds himself unable to punish Tuptim he insists, "I am King, as I was born to be, and Siam is to be governed in my way! . . . Not English way, not French way, not Chinese way. My way!"

Explain to students the distinction sociologist Peter Berger draws between the traditional value of honor derived from one's status or standing in society and the modern notion of innate human dignity.[9] Ask them to consider, in light of how the play ends, the extent to which each of these values enters the king's inner conflict. Ask them what assumptions might lie behind the traditional English expression "The king is dead. Long live the king." Ask them who dies at the end of this play, the king, a man, or both.

---

9. Peter Berger, Brigitte Berger, and Hansfried Kellner, *The Homeless Mind: Modernization and Consciousness* (New York: Random House, 1973).

Much of the comedy in *The King and I* derives from the practice of deference, of bowing to pay homage to the king. Much of the commentary in the play comes from the sons of the two principals, remarking on the confusion of their parents. Indeed Peter Berger notes that the transition from traditional to modern societies involves the diminishing of what young people can learn by imitating their elders, the expansion of what they must learn by themselves and from each other.[10] In the final scene of *The King and I* the Kralahome crouches low near the deathbed of the king, while the king's son, the new king, stands erect, making a decree abolishing the "custom of bowing to King in fashion of lowly toad." His father's last words underline the predicament of those caught in the transition from traditional to modern societies. "It has been said there shall be no bowing for showing respect of King. It has been said by one who has . . . been trained for royal government." As a concluding assignment, ask the students to re-read the play, or to attend the production in their school, and then write a brief essay about what the new king might learn concerning the modern world, not from Anna, but from the experiences of his father. Ask them to include some thoughts about how the new king should provide for the education of his own children. The assignment will provide students both with the opportunity to think further about how "modern societies function and how they have developed" and with a chance to reflect on their own educations in the context of this process.

Eveline

Our second illustration deals with including a short story by James Joyce in the study of migration discussed in Chapter 3. The story is entitled "Eveline" and is part of the collection of stories known as the *Dubliners* (see Appendix B for a reprint of the story).[11] It is simply written, only a few pages in length, and can be read by a student in one, brief sitting. The story is intended to be a faithful

---

10. Ibid.

11. James Joyce, *Dubliners* (Harmondsworth, Middlesex: Penguin Books, 1956).

rendering of the thoughts and feelings of a young Irish girl, about 19 years old, who pauses for a moment to consider her actions a few hours before she is to migrate to Argentina. The time is near the turn of the last century. The opportunity to leave Dublin has come through a proposal of marriage, but now, in the evening of the night on which she is to sail, she grows less sure of her decision to depart. Through most of the story, Eveline sits looking from her window into the street and around the room at "those familiar objects from which [previously] she had never dreamed of being divided."

A question presses upon her: "She had consented to go away, to leave her home. Was that wise?" Considering this question with her takes students directly and dramatically into a central problem of migration—the choice of going or staying. Close attention to how she responds to the situation can illuminate student thinking about why so many left one land for another, and also why so many others who might have gone remained where they were. In addition, such material makes study less general and helps picture "the usually anonymous individual migrant."[12] In doing so, it also permits students to view someone near their own age as a historical actor, as someone who has reached a personal turning point within what is also a part of a large historical process.

Discussion of this reading might proceed in a number of ways and address a variety of questions. The activity, however, should probably take place near the conclusion of the study of migration. Then students can apply their acquired knowledge to Eveline's dilemma and profit from the recognitions previous learning brings to reading the story. For example, teachers might ask students to identify and briefly discuss major elements of Eveline's social and cultural setting that bear on the issue of migration. An acquired social history perspective should enable them to notice factors of religion, of family and gender, and of community and neighborhood—and, moreover, to notice them less as abstractions than as aspects of Eveline's personal circumstances and identity.

---

12. Frank Thistlethwaite, "Migration from Europe Overseas in the Nineteenth and Twentieth Centuries." In Stanley N. Katz and Stanley I. Kutler (eds.), *New Perspectives on the American Past*, vol. 2, *1877 to the Present* (Boston: Little, Brown, 1969) p. 59.

Class discussions might begin with the teacher helping students to assemble information about Eveline conveyed through details in the story. Attention might fall first on how much information can be gleaned from the physical objects in the room—from, say, the photograph of the priest hanging on the wall. Here students might be encouraged to contrast past and present by comparing these objects with those in their own homes or the homes of acquaintances. What change (and what continuity), for instance, may be suggested by the prevalence of posters featuring rock performers or media stars in the current scene? Attention to the physical objects also should include notice of their condition, for example, that the photograph of the priest is "yellowing" and the harmonium is "broken." An open discussion of this sort should begin to alert students to the wealth of information available to them regarding Eveline's historical and social situation.

Attention might next turn to Eveline's relations with people. Students will probably mention first that Eveline's father looms very large in her thoughts. They may, in fact, find this the occasion for some sarcasm. Still, this is an opportunity to explore historical generalizations about paternal authority in a traditional society and to trace the controlling reach of the father in some detail in every aspect of Eveline's existence. Work, earnings, marriage, conscience, and time itself—all and more we see are touched in what in this case is a hard and confining rule. At this point, the teacher may choose to give students a rather loose rein if they draw contrasts with their own situations.

Having opened the story in this way to historical inquiry, the teacher might then ask students to turn more systematically to a consideration of cause and effect, "push" and "pull" factors, in Eveline's anticipated departure. Not only the father, but poverty, grinding routine, and lack of any prospect for change join to make a "hard life" and prompt Eveline to look away from Dublin when the chance comes; hope of social "respect" and the exhilarating idea of freedom in "another life" draw her toward Buenos Aires. Discussion at this point might speculate on what a new life means for Eveline and what kind of elements enter into her idea of social respect. The talk here should touch on how marriage confers status upon women in traditional societies and how this differs from the current situation in modern societies. This can then lead to consideration of which of the factors—"push" or "pull"—seem more specific, more concrete; and how conclusions about this support or disagree with the historian Robert Cross's statement that most migrants "leave a place because they are uncomfortable where they are" rather than because of the attraction of some destination.[13] In moving toward a momentary pause, the teacher might ask students to reflect tentatively on how their conclusions on this point revise or confirm their view of the history of immigration to the United States and other countries developed in previous study.

The story provides other opportunities for students to test historical hypotheses in a limited way through details provided in the tale. For instance, one view of migration argues that migrants leave a place not just because of its rigidities and limitations, but also because important changes have already begun to alter the *status quo* in the home situation. The continuation of change in the midst of continuity may create perplexing issues about the future and also raises questions of choice that previously did not exist. What of the scene from her window in this regard? The field in which she played as a child has been turned into a housing development— "not like their little brown houses, but bright brick houses with shining roofs." And many people she once knew have come and gone. How do these and other changes bring her, at least momentarily, to the conclusion that "Everything changes" and contribute to the idea that she too will "go away like the others, . . . leave her home"?

Discussion of these questions can lead to further consideration of how factors of change and persistence combine to give urgency to Eveline's decision. Analysis might continue to focus on her social status. Is it stable or declining? Do the "new red houses" of the neighborhood present threat or opportunity? What about the family structure? She has pledged "to keep the home together," but is it as unchanged or unchanging as might be implied by her thoughts about the "familiar objects which she had dusted once a week for so many years"? Responding to questions such as these can help

---

13. Robert D. Cross, "American Society: 1865-1914." In John A. Garraty (ed.), *Interpreting American History: Conversations with Historians, Part II* (New York: Macmillan, 1970), p. 33.

students achieve recognition that history should not be regarded as an impersonal laundry list of cause and effect factors, but rather must be thought of more dramatically as the interaction, and often conflict, of historical elements in the shaping of human lives.

And what of the steamship that waits to carry Eveline across the Atlantic? In previous study, students will have considered the historical change from traditional to modern forms of society, including the part played in this transformation by technological advances in transportation and communication. Through Eveline's case, they can ask how technical improvements altered choices open to individuals and changed the questions people asked about their lot in life. We often think of travel as the province of the rich, and yet historians now recognize that, by the nineteenth century, laborers in large numbers had begun to journey about the world in search of work opportunities and economic improvement. As one authority puts it:

> It is possible that if records of such movements were to be gathered they would reveal an amazing frequency of proletarian globe-trotting, a frequency unequalled by the upper-class traveller of the richer countries.[14]

Still, the angle of vision is hard to reverse. When the *Titanic* was recently discovered at the bottom of the Atlantic, newspapers once again emphasized how such great steamships were the playgrounds of the rich and fashionable. Journalistic accounts made a point of noting that ten millionaires went down with the vessel. And yet, we know that the fortunes of the major shipping companies from Cunard and Austro-American to the modern Greek lines have been based, not upon a wealthy elite, but upon emigrants. It is the poor emigrant who made up the "valuable bulk cargo" that made these shipping concerns economically viable.

A major focus of discussion, of course, must be Eveline's drawing back from her decision to leave and her final anguished inability to

---

14. R. F. Foerster, *Italian Emigration of Our Times* (1919), p. 37, cited in Frank Thistlethwaite, "Migration from Europe Overseas in the Nineteenth and Twentieth Centuries." In Stanley N. Katz and Stanley I. Kutler (eds.), *New Perspectives on the American Past*, p. 63.

board the ship. "No! No! No! It was impossible." There are a number of ways to regard this change of mind (note that she had already written letters to her father and brother explaining her departure). One must involve consideration of the risks entailed in migration. We see that the things of her everyday life begin to appear somewhat less grim when weighed against an uncertain future in "a distant unknown country." Indeed, Eveline must face very basic considerations. "In her home anyway she had shelter and food; she had those whom she had known all her life about her." In the new place she could not be sure of anything, even that necessities for life could be found. From this perspective, her present situation, hard as it is, does not seem "a wholly undesirable life." Her increasing trepidation is our opportunity for increasing historical understanding. Our own national legend, perhaps too much, takes for granted the idea of migration as a path to social improvement and does not comprehend its serious risks, its many actual difficulties and defeats. Could not uprooting be equally, and maybe more, harrowing than remaining in a distressing situation? In leaving, what security does Eveline surrender? What connections does she break and what values does she call into question? How, in fact, is the whole structure of her life shaken? And, finally, is it clear that she will be "better off" for having ventured such radical change? Here discussion should return to information presented in the previous study of migration, which suggests that large numbers of immigrants re-emigrated (for example, that perhaps as many as a third of the immigrants to the United States in the century before the end of World War I returned to their homeland). This can result in a review of different motives at play in migration and discussion of how these might influence questions of repatriation.

A simple approach to envisioning Eveline's situation in historical perspective could be to ask half the class to defend Eveline's final action and the other half to argue against it. In advance of the discussion, each student should prepare a short paper developing the side of the question assigned to his or her group. Preparation of the paper will give each student practice in appraising Joyce's historical vision of Eveline's case, either criticizing or supporting it, and in developing a historical interpretation of his or her own. It also will give them practice in historical writing, and each paper should be collected and marked with an eye to helping individual students with their written work. Social studies teachers can benefit in this activity from perusal of the description of the writing process in *Academic Preparation in English*. In-class discussion of the papers can make vivid the conflict that Eveline experienced, and at the same time illuminate the integrity of arguments on each side of the question. In spirit, discussion should avoid what E. P. Thompson called the "enormous condescension of posterity"[15]— that is, remembering with favor only those who anticipated in their behavior what we now believe, or take for granted, to be the course history has marked as successful. Eveline said no to migration. So did others who had opportunity and choice. We can comment on their actions, but remembering that it was they, not we, who bore the consequences of choice in their own lives and time.

One possible difficulty in this discussion can be turned to opportunity. Members of the class will point out that the writer of this story appears to view Eveline's final action, her staying rather than going, as a failure of some kind. The teacher then can mention that Joyce himself was an emigrant, or perhaps more properly, an "exile"—that he lived most of his adult life in Zurich and Paris at least in part as a protest against life in Dublin. This might deepen the discussion of different ways people leave the land of their birth and take up life in another country. Teachers can ask students to explore the meaning of "expatriate" or the definition of "resident alien" in our immigration codes. All this can contribute not only to a discussion of how the weight of this particular story falls, but also to how writings about migration are seldom entirely disinterested or "value free." The teacher might point out, for example, that histories written from a national point of view frequently mention immigration but almost never take up the subject of emigration. Conversation about why this might be so can lead to insight about the part that feelings and values play in the making of historical interpretations.

This classroom activity also illustrates how history serves to synthesize knowledge across the curriculum. Study of "Eveline" from a historical perspective brings together social science concepts and material from the humanities. Moreover, it involves students in

---

15. Edward P. Thompson, *The Making of the English Working Class* (New York: Random House, 1966).

seeing history from "the bottom up"—the angle of vision opened by social history. In this case, they "see" migration through the perceptions of a young girl, unnoteworthy in the realm of politics and rulers, but who nevertheless lived in the midst of choice and conflict created by large historical processes.

Attention to Eveline's youth also can help focus important interrelations among factors in such processes. Social history has included the young as a social group in its range of concerns and asked about the importance of generational relations in historical change. Indeed, Kammen points out that this "one thematic emphasis has pervaded and affected nearly all the subdisciplines of historical writing in the United States during the past decade."[16] Students need not be deeply acquainted with current scholarship to discover the force of this theme in Eveline's story. We already have mentioned conflict with her father, but what of her ties to her mother? Students may want to explore how Eveline's perceptions of her mother contributed to ambivalence regarding change in her own life, and this can lead to discussion of how the readiness or resistance of one generation to repeat the way of life of another enters into the problem of change over time.

This exploration can return discussion to questions about the factor of age in migration more generally. Previous study will have provided some data on this point—perhaps that 75 percent, and probably more, of the total immigrant flow to the United States between 1865 and 1914 was between 18 and 39 years of age. Most figures, in fact, indicate that immigrants were overwhelmingly young, the large majority being of the family-forming, child-rearing age. Students might ask what effect this could produce in the receiving country, but also what it might mean for the country left behind. Under what conditions would it help or harm to lose so much youth and energy from the population and how might this affect the historical development of a country? These are complex questions with no definite answers, but asking them can help students understand once again that how one views this process often

16. Michael Kammen (ed.), "Introduction: The Historian's Vocation and the State of the Discipline in the United States," in *The Past Before Us: Contemporary Historical Writing in the United States* (Ithaca, New York: Cornell University Press, 1980), p. 37.

depends on where one stands in relation to it. Finally, however, it underlines how historical processes in their causes and effects, costs and gains, reciprocally join parts of the globe that are far removed geographically and very different from one another in language, culture, and outlook.

Of the Sorrow Songs

The two previous activities require time to carry out, but strengthen study overall by giving students opportunities to practice historical thought in some depth and detail. It may be, moreover, that pressures on classroom time are not so great as often assumed. For instance, eleventh-grade United States history textbooks generally cover the same periods and repeat much of the same information as presented in eighth-grade texts.[17] Slavish adherence to texts, then, can result in unproductive repetition and lead students to think of history as a rehash of familiar facts. Good use of historical materials from outside the text not only provides time for skills development, but also opens a window through which different aspects of content can be viewed.

We can use the total time available in the curriculum to better effect. Thinking of study in small units or as totally discrete parts may conceal how major elements of the curriculum can relate to one another and how building upon, as well as varying, learning can lead to greater cumulative student achievement in both skills development and knowledge acquisition. The twelfth-grade social science teacher, for instance, can build upon the social history emphasis of previous courses to broaden student perspective on American political experience and behavior.

Social history, as noted, extends study to the historical experience of ordinary citizens and especially to the powerless among them. This approach takes political behavior to include both the pursuit and exercise of power, and the response and adjustment to power of people or groups who are subject to it. Such an angle of

---

17. Douglas D. Alder and Matthew T. Downey, "Problem Areas in the History Curriculum." In Matthew T. Downey (ed.), *History in the Schools* (Washington, D.C.: National Council for the Social Studies, 1985), p. 19.

vision, therefore, allows students to see the attempts of oppressed and minority groups to retain cohesion and some control over their own affairs as an important part of political life. Equally important, it helps them to understand that the relative failure or success of these attempts does not necessarily diminish or increase their significance—as, say, is usually the case in national presidential campaigns.

Such a perspective also encourages further consideration of materials and sources other than textbooks. How do social scientists and historians glimpse the thoughts and feelings of "the oppressed, the inarticulate, the marginal"? These are groups that do not ordinarily leave testimony conveniently on library shelves. Indeed, a leading symptom of their powerlessness may be their lack of means and opportunity to express themselves. In indicating to students the ways in which social scientists have approached this problem, teachers can illustrate how inquiry advances by means of ideas drawn from several social sciences. For example, study of the "plebeian" political culture of Europe currently relies heavily on an anthropological mode of understanding to decipher possible political meanings in folk rituals, festivals, and music.

To create opportunities for discussion, teachers might introduce work in which social scientists have made telling use of source materials. By twelfth grade, students should be reading some commentaries by social scientists on subjects or issues under discussion. This is important not so much to add to the student's stock of information as to provide experience with diverse approaches and interpretations. These readings can be selected in such a way as not only to bear on the matter under study, but also to provide simple, but effective examples of the use of sources other than customary written records. In discussion, teachers can point out to students considerations in the use of source materials, and help them recognize the ways other sources lead to discovery.

For example, the twelfth-grade social science course often takes up the political experience of black Americans. The impact of slavery and segregation in American political history makes this a logical curricular decision, but many of the same points would emerge in studying labor groups or the experience of such minorities as Native Americans and Hispanics. In studying the experience of black Americans, a teacher might assign selected readings from

W. E. B. Du Bois's *The Souls of Black Folk*.[18] This work of an eminent sociologist, first published in 1903 and still basic reading in its subject, is both an interesting example of inquiry and an important historical and political document in itself. Moreover, the final chapter of the book entitled "Of the Sorrow Songs" provides a brief but striking example of how sources can make a difference in understanding.

The book, though many things, is specifically an urgently reasoned protest against failures in this country to deliver on the promise of political and civil liberties pledged to blacks at the close of the Civil War and, indeed, against an increasing curtailment of such liberties as blacks had briefly gained. This growing resistance relied, in part, on the historical argument that blacks were more content in the condition of slavery than in freedom—"that life was joyous to the black slave, careless and happy." Absurd as this seems now, it was a powerful assumption at the time and one difficult to refute because slaves had been denied all means and opportunity to speak for themselves, hence to leave records that told a different story.

But, Du Bois points out that the silence was not complete. Slaves "sang songs in the olden days . . . for they were weary at heart." He follows with a discussion of the folk songs, many of which will still be familiar to students today. They include "Nobody Knows the Trouble I've Seen," "Swing Low, Sweet Chariot," and "Steal Away." Du Bois conveys that whatever face the slave may have shown in the midst of oppression, "their songs are the articulate message of the slave to the world." And however strong the assumption might be to the contrary, no listener can deny that this "music is distinctly sorrowful."

Moreover, students' own acquaintance with this music (and with popular music generally) may help them see that the force of this source is not in the message alone. The power of Du Bois's statement also comes from his ability to show how familiar things have not been rightly understood. They can follow as Du Bois rehearses how well his readers know these songs, how thoroughly they have "passed into current airs." The way audiences have heard them

---

18. W. E. B. Du Bois, *The Souls of Black Folk* (New York: New American Library, 1969).

may vary, ranging from the "debasements and imitations" of the minstrel stage to their true and triumphant performance by the Fisk Jubilee Singers. But the point is that the slave experience did not go unspoken. Indeed, it had been widely broadcast in these songs and, ironically, much applauded. If people had not heard the true message, it is because they somehow had chosen not to listen.

Teachers can use this discussion to talk about how folk expressions, though usually simple on the surface, are often rich and complex in what they contain. Performed and transmitted from generation to generation over long stretches of time, they take into themselves "the siftings of centuries." Du Bois finds in these songs not only signs of African origins, but also the graftings of Christian theology and intrusions of the "cant phrases" of popular entertainment. This makes a small number of songs into a "forest of melody."

The scrutiny of sources, however, should assist, not detract from, the search into the songs' essential meanings. Indeed, technical knowledge of music is not needed to find in these songs how black slaves felt about many things. Attitudes toward nature and work are present and performed in them; so are feelings regarding death, about which the slave "showed little fear." Moreover, they force further questions upon the listener. This comes from things we might expect to hear when we genuinely listen, but do not, from questions that come to mind because of "eloquent omissions and silences." Du Bois anticipates and helps form many critical issues of modern social science when he says of these songs: "Mother and child are sung, but seldom father; fugitive and weary wanderer call for pity and affection, but there is little of wooing and wedding; the rocks and the mountains are well known, but home is unknown." Perhaps there is no better statement from which to begin consideration of social sciences' now long, sustained attempt to understand the impact of the experience of slavery on the black family.

But the major social and political point is left in no doubt in this music. The slave lived in the "shadow of fear" and much of what he expressed in any form had to be "veiled." Nevertheless, no historical interpretation of the slave experience can deny the essential message of these songs and argue that the slave did not protest his condition and long to escape from it. In many voices, Du Bois says, they present the same testimony. "They are the music of an unhappy people, of the children of disappointment; they tell of death and suffering and unvoiced longing toward a truer world, of misty wanderings and hidden ways." This statement of "longing" is no less political for lacking a specific vision of the future. By introducing a reading like "Of the Sorrow Songs" into a twelfth-grade course on American political behavior, a teacher can provide students with needed experience in making direct use of the work of social scientists. Moreover, students will have the opportunity to bring their previous learning in history courses to bear as they begin to think deeply about the concept of power and the related conditions of powerlessness.

V. Social Studies and the Basic Academic Competencies

The study of history and the social sciences provides high school students with an extraordinarily broad range of opportunities to develop the Basic Academic Competencies outlined in *Academic Preparation for College*. Those competencies are reading, writing, speaking and listening, mathematics, reasoning, studying, computer competency, and observing. And yet, perhaps more than their colleagues in English and mathematics departments, for example, social studies teachers often can be reluctant to acknowledge these opportunities. Perhaps we fear that concern for such general intellectual skills will detract from the importance of our subject matter in its own right, and, in truth, this sometimes can be a danger. But the further truth is that the historical skills and ways of developing them that we discussed in Chapters 3 and 4 are of a piece with the Basic Academic Competencies. To take just one example, but a central one, those historical skills are summarized by the general statement that students will need "some understanding of how to approach the problem of change over time." The first reasoning competency listed in *Academic Preparation for College* is "the ability to identify and formulate problems, as well as the ability to propose and evaluate ways to solve them." Just as in the case of the statements of historical skills, however, such abstract discussion is less convincing and far less useful than actually showing how the Basic Academic Competencies operate and are developed as students address real historical problems. Consequently, this chapter explores the Basic Academic Competencies by suggesting how teachers might approach investigation of such a problem. We hope that you will find the problem itself interesting, for that will be one indication of the accuracy of our conviction that exercise of the Basic Academic Competencies can—and should—be intrinsic to the study of history and the social sciences, not a distraction from it.

We choose an illustration drawn from American social history between World War I and World War II for an important reason. Choice of this period of American history provides the opportunity to work with a form of historical information we have not yet discussed: film. We prefer to use film, as other newer technologies, for the unique possibilities it brings in itself rather than as a substitute for other forms of teaching and learning. We like to use films that are genuine products of a previous time, and windows on that time, rather than films that are simply alternate forms of textbooks and lectures. In the case of the period between World War I and World War II, film has the further advantage of being central to American culture. One high school history textbook points out that by the 1920s the movie industry had become the fourth largest in the country.[1] The first successful motion picture with sound appeared in 1927 and one scholar, Warren Sussman, has noted that this and related inventions "created an exceptional world of sound: a culture transported through the telephone, phonograph, radio, and talking pictures."[2]

Much of historical study begins with trying to grasp what the past has to express. Thus in Chapter 4 we explored how other kinds of readings might be used to supplement the textbook. Our point is not that reading textbooks and listening to lectures ought to be ignored in the high school study of history, but rather that the more ways in which students are able to grasp and formulate a knowledge of history, the more likely they are to understand it well. Similar points are made in the fifth chapters of this book's companions in mathematics, the arts, and English. Working with film provides an opportunity to apprehend the past not by means of reading but with experience in another of what linguists call the receptive skills. Since the social studies statement in *Academic Preparation for College* calls attention to visual forms of information, and since such forms of communication are increasingly important in our own time, it seems worthwhile to begin to develop a vision of American

1. Carol Berkin and Leonard Wood, *Land of Promise: A History of the United States from 1865* (Glenview, Illinois: Scott, Foresman, 1983), p. 216.

2. Warren Sussman, *Culture as History: The Transformation of American Society in the Twentieth Century* (New York: Pantheon Books, 1984), p. xxv.

culture in the 1930s with an exercise in what unfortunately is still a neglected competency: observing.

This competency bears some resemblances to the other receptive skills, and an initial showing of director Frank Capra's 1934 film *It Happened One Night* might engage students in a level of observation that in reading is called scanning. They observe the film to get a general overview but also with an eye to specific information. Students might be asked to attend particularly to the persons in the film and to the relations among them. A teacher might ask students to jot brief notes on when various characters appear and on notable exchanges between them. At this stage, however, greater emphasis should be given to acquiring a general overview of the film.

The focus on characters in the film will be useful because it will lead the ensuing discussion to a consideration of the plot of the film, a matter that will preoccupy students in any case. Ask which main character is presented first in the film. This will help establish that the film follows Ellie Andrews, a rich young woman whose marriage to a celebrity aviator her father is trying to break up and have annulled. The question also will focus prompt attention on Peter Warne, an arrogant young newspaperman who accompanies Ellie Andrews as she tries to elude her father and return to her new husband.

Asking about the relations among these characters very likely will elicit some confusion because those relations change in the course of the film. Gradually students will sort out those changing relations in the plot: Ellie Andrews changes from hostility toward Peter Warne to ultimately falling in love with him; Peter Warne changes from trying to get a newspaper story out of Ellie's escape to being in love with her. In the process, Ellie stops opposing her father's opinion of King Wesly, the aviator, and comes to agree with that opinion.

With this much established, it is none too soon to ask students a question concerning the title of the film: "To what night does the title refer? What happened then?" High school students are likely to lavish a great deal of attention and comment on the final scene of the film in which, marriage between Ellie and Peter having been assured, the sexual "wall of Jericho" that they had maintained between them is said to be toppling. Posing the question about the title as part of a discussion about changing relations among the various characters in the film will help the students distinguish between their own reaction and the film's intention. Ultimately some will identify the night in question as the scene in the hayfield in which Ellie and Peter first begin to speak directly to one another and fall in love.

High school students probably will also have a good deal to say about the 1930s slang used by characters in the film. A little advance preparation by a teacher can take advantage of this interest and begin to move students more deeply into the historical world recreated or imagined in the film. Make a list of several of the most striking of these slang expressions: mug, jam, 5 G's, rod, sucker. It will form the basis for a writing exercise that can contribute to students' understanding of language and to all the Basic Academic Competencies based on language. As a preparation for the exercise ask the students to recall which characters used such slang (notably Peter Warne and Oscar Shapely, a disagreeable traveling salesman). Now get into the writing exercise by asking the students if they know what the slang expressions mean. Ask each student to write out a definition for each term. When that is completed—it is likely to be a surprisingly perplexing task—ask the students to add to each definition an equivalent expression in today's slang. When the writing exercise is completed, ask several students to read aloud the definitions and equivalent expressions they have given for one of the original slang expressions. As the discussion moves from one expression to another, many students may be eager to join in with alternatives and comments.

This exercise is likely to be a good deal of fun for all concerned but it also will go a long way toward establishing some serious points about language and history. Asking for both definitions and equivalent slang expressions can make clear to students the point made in the English statement in *Academic Preparation for College* that "English has several levels of usage, and consequently the language appropriate in some situations may not be appropriate in others." The effectiveness of the different levels of usage in the film will help extend this point to one made in the Basic Academic Competency statements on both writing and speaking concerning the importance of being able to vary one's use of written and spoken language. Indeed, the writing exercise will have given the students experience in doing just that.

A second point that this exercise can help students understand also is made in the English statement about language: "English continues to undergo change." We have mentioned several times that a fundamental problem in teaching history is to help students come to grips with the "otherness" of the past, with how different previous times and societies really were. Once such differences sink in, the work of understanding the past gets under way in earnest. The opposite side of this coin is that many aspects of the past are not recognized as such because they are so familiar. For many students *It Happened One Night* will not be part of the cultural history of the 1930s, but something they can rent at their local videocassette store. An exercise that draws attention to how American language has changed over time will help put the film at the "proper distance," and will help students identify the film as presenting a problem, the problem of change over time.

Many students will get quite playful while coming up with the slang equivalents in the writing exercise. This very inventiveness will help establish a third important point, this one dealing directly with the nature of the relations among the various people in the film. The earlier question about who uses slang in the film can be emphasized by asking the reverse: "Who does not use slang?" Students will note that while Peter Warne talks that way, Ellie Andrews does not. The point can be underlined by recalling the scene in which she tries to deal, in her own linguistic manner, with the obnoxious and slang advances of Oscar Shapely. That both Shapely and Peter Warne use slang, even though they are quite different characters, will help establish what students probably noticed early on: that slang is used by a certain kind of person in the film and that part of the answer to the question about relations among people in the film is that it involves relations between rich and common people. This is no moment to be preachy about "correct" English, however, because director Frank Capra and writer Robert Riskin are celebrating common people. Much of what makes Peter Warne so winning is his resourcefulness, his inventiveness, his ingenuity, in language as in other things. The very playfulness in language that students might enjoy in discussing their writing exercise may help them appreciate one characteristic the film values in ordinary people.

A teacher might inquire how the students knew that Ellie Andrews was rich and that Peter Warne was a reporter. One ready answer would be that she was first encountered on a yacht and he was first seen talking to his editor from a telephone booth. This sort of observation prepares the way for a more structured exercise in observing that will move students much more deeply both into the film and into American culture of the 1930s. A teacher might note that the students' response involved things rather than persons and observe that this was an aspect of the film that had not yet been considered. Divide the class into three groups and ask the students to observe the film again, this time keeping a tally of a certain aspect of what they observe. Ask students in one group to make lists of all the striking or important *things* or *objects* in the film. Ask those in another group to list all the different kinds of *places* in the film. Ask those in the third group to keep track of all the *sounds,* other than conversations between people, that they hear in the film. If it is more convenient, teachers may want to create six groups and divide observation of the film in half at the "One Night" scene. This could help stress that students are not simply being asked to watch a movie for a second time, but to carry out methodical observation and analysis.

After the observation has been completed, work with each group to compile master lists of things, places, and sounds. With these compilations the exercise in observation becomes one in reasoning, particularly in induction and forming generalizations. Ask the students to determine if any of the items on the list of things have anything in common. At this point Warren Sussman's observation about the kinds of things featured in the film and how they represent meaning will virtually leap out at the students. "There is virtually no known means of communication left unexploited iconographically in the film: telegrams, radios, police calls, newspapers and newspaper headlines, newsreel cameras and cameramen, photographs, telephones (often in a crucial role and generally leading to misunderstanding), police cars and motorcycles, typewriters. There is every kind of car from Model T to limousine."[3] By classifying the objects they have listed, students will observe that an extraordinary proportion of the objects in the film are used either to convey

---

3. Ibid., pp. 265-266.

messages (telephone, newspaper, radio) or to convey people themselves (bus, airplane, automobile).

Turning students' attention to the places in the film will confirm this finding. The students' tallies will show that a high proportion of the important places in the film are either means of transportation themselves (yacht, bus, airplane, automobile) or closely associated with the new means of transportation and communication: bus station; autocamp; roadside diner; an office full of intercoms, telephones, and teletypes; even a lawn that becomes the launching pad for an autogyro and an automobile.

Similarly, analysis of the list of sounds will emphasize the film's preoccupation with the new means of transportation and communication that had become widespread in American society of the 1930s. Sorting out the kinds of things actually heard will make it seem that the film had been scored largely for engines, typewriters, and telephone bells, although students also will note voices raised in song (on the bus) and the pastoral sounds of the "One Night" scene in the hayfield. That the latter are counterpointed by a lonely, distant train whistle will perhaps underline the pivotal role of this scene in the film.

A teacher might extend this simple quantitative analysis of the film by recalling that the conversation of ordinary people is set off clearly in the film and asking if the material things in the film also are associated with rich or ordinary people. Some cases will be clear (airplanes and buses, radios and newspapers); others will be less so (telephones, railroads). In any case, this exercise in systematic observation and generalization will help students see that in addition to the film's manifest plot, it also is engrossed with the means of communication and transportation that had proliferated in the America of the 1930s. Moreover, relating things to people will begin to alert students to the film's exploration of how new technology creates new social situations and changes the textures of social life.

The question about the relation of the material things to ordinary or rich people will have prepared the students for a fuller exercise in bringing together their now quite detailed information concerning the film. This calls for work in a different kind of reasoning, one that involves interpretation or synthesis, showing how different kinds of things are related or interact. This sort of reasoning is crucial in historical work because it involves assembling information about the past into a plausible reconstruction of some previous situation or episode. Ordinarily such reasoning takes place in conjunction with writing, particularly the prewriting stage of arranging information and ideas before the actual setting down of words on paper. While many teachers in various subjects have come to appreciate the importance of prewriting, the value of a similar stage in preparing for speaking—the other productive competency—is less widely recognized. The following exercise leads students toward the integration of information about the film while developing what *Academic Preparation for College* calls "the ability to conceive and develop ideas about a topic for the purpose of speaking to a group; to choose and organize related ideas. . . ."

To set the exercise in motion, a teacher might recall that the film introduces Ellie Andrews first and thereby encourages viewers to attend to her point of view. Moreover, the teacher might note that in the course of the film Ellie changes a great deal. At its beginning she is a rather helpless young woman who encounters all sorts of obstacles in her journey to her love. Her love is not so much a person as a way of life—Ellie calls it a merry-go-round, students might call it "the fast lane." Or some students might suggest that her concerns are more with escaping from a current life than in knowing what she wants from a new one. In any case, by the end of the film Ellie is able to break out of her circumstances—a second wedding to the celebrity aviator—and flee successfully to the very different man she now loves. In the course of these changes Ellie becomes a woman whom Peter no longer sees as a "story" but as someone "who is real, who is alive," as someone he loves. Ask students to prepare a three- or four-minute talk on how, in the course of the film, Ellie learns to deal with the situations that surround her.

A first step might be to divide the class into small discussion groups. Just as it is important in prewriting that students begin to get some words down on paper, so it is important in preparing an oral presentation that students begin to speak, to express what they have in mind. Ask each group to review their lists of things and identify which presented problems, which hindered Ellie on her journey. Students' attention quickly will fall on the episode in which the bus leaves the station without her, even though she assumed the driver would wait for her. Not even rich young women can always stop the buses from running on time. This line of discovery may be extended to include the means of transportation and communication that assisted her father in his attempt to prevent her escape to speed ahead of her. In seeing how Ellie is confronted by these technological circumstances students also may glimpse the situation of many Americans in the 1930s.

Now broaden the range of information students are to synthesize. Ask the groups to refer to their notes on characters in the film and select some people as well as things that have either hindered or helped Ellie on her journey. Ask how these interactions lead her to change, and what she learns from them. Students will note, among many other episodes, the advances of Oscar Shapely and the inventiveness of Peter Warne in shielding Ellie Andrews by saying that she was his wife. That Ellie learns this inventiveness may be suggested by a later scene in which she and Peter deceive detectives by acting like a poor country couple. That she learns limits to such inventiveness may be indicated by the famous hitchhiking scene and subsequent diner scene in which Peter conveys his disapproval of "gold-digging." The point, of course, is not to suggest interpretations to the students, but to create a situation in which they can begin to reorganize the information and impressions they have gathered and to express new relations among them. Do not try to draw the discussions to any conclusions but instead give the students more details on their assignment for the next day. Ask them to outline, on a single piece of paper, a three- or four-minute presentation in which they answer the following questions:

1. How did Ellie Andrews realize that she had a problem in completing her journey?
2. How did she attempt to solve her problem?
3. What attempts failed? What worked?
4. What attracted her to Peter Warne? What attracted him to her?

The next day do not attempt to have every student give a presentation. Be sure to collect all the outlines, but after three or four students from different groups have made their presentations, allow the entire class to join in the discussion. This is the moment of synthesis and all the students will have prepared something to contribute. It is worth remarking that it is as important to be fully prepared for a discussion as it is for a formal presentation.

Having assembled some meaning from the film, the students are in a good position to begin thinking about the film in its larger context—American culture and society in the 1930s. Recall the impoverished mother on the bus and the boxcar-riding "hoboes" the students saw in the film. Remind them about what they read in their textbooks concerning the Great Depression, but observe that *It Happened One Night* implies a "happily ever after" conclusion. Note also that the end of the film finds Ellie and Peter still on the road, likely to encounter more obstacles, and required to invent new ways of dealing with them. Here is an opportunity to make an important observation about the nature of the evidence students have been examining. Although films (and even some history courses) seem to progress smoothly toward some end, real life continues on, open-ended, with many ups and downs. Ask if the viewers of the film in the 1930s were likely to share in the film's general optimism and high spirits. Note that the filmmakers were aware of audience feelings and ask students to consider how this may have influenced their decision about matters of plot and tone.

This can lead to a discussion of possible "escapist" tendencies in the film. Speculate that such tendencies may run deep both in the film and in American culture. What, for example, is Peter Warne's idea of "the good life"? Could his statements about a happy state lead to what Huck Finn called "lighting out for the territory"? Given the chance, where does he propose to live with Ellie? Is it in any of the places and societies shown in the film or is it elsewhere? Note in this connection his talk about living on an isolated Pacific island and that he and Ellie honeymoon somewhere in the Michigan wilderness. This can lead students to speculate about what has been called the American penchant for "moving on." Here a connection can be made with the study of migration discussed in Chapters 3 and 4. Much of our history begins with immigration and continues in movement of one kind or another. This inclination to move, some argue, can be an evasion of social responsibility or even an end in itself. "To many Americans," Sussman says, "movement in space was the equivalent of social mobility."[4]

With this as additional background, we can ask students to un-

---

4. Ibid., p. 263.

dertake a concluding assignment. Recall with them that in the course of the film Peter Warne wrote a newspaper story about the journey of Ellie Andrews. This story was discarded in a moment of seeming defeat, but the implication remains that Warne's account contains the truth. Somewhere in this account we can imagine that he would have described a moment when things seemed as they should be—when Ellie, and he, and the other characters felt especially good about themselves and the world in which they lived. Ask the students to review their notes and then write a short newspaper story, giving the when, where, who, what, and why that fully describes this moment. Remind them also to consider particularly as they write how the moment selected speaks to the concerns and interests of the American reading public of the 1930s. The reporter Peter Warne would have had this audience much in mind as *he* wrote, of course. This assignment gives students practice both in thinking their way into a historical situation and in developing the writing competence described in *Academic Preparation for College* as the "ability to write appropriately for different occasions, audiences, and purposes."

Some students, of course, still will choose to write about the final scene of the film. Others, however, may select a less conclusive moment—a time perhaps when the good life was briefly glimpsed, or momentarily held, but which did not last except as an ideal in the mind. Reviewing the list of episodes, some will write about the "One Night" in the hayfield when Ellie and Peter step outside the world of technological interference and begin to communicate frankly and directly. Others might write about the night in the autocamp outside Philadelphia when Ellie and Peter begin to share a dream about escaping to an island. Students who have felt the force of technology in the film might write about the exhilaration Ellie must have felt when she disrupted that second wedding and used an automobile to go off after Peter Warne. Others might write about the scene in which a whole group of passengers, including Ellie and Peter, join in song, momentarily in harmony with one another on the bus. The point is not for the students to agree on an answer, but that—as we suggested at the end of Chapter 3—students draw more and more of what they have learned into a fuller and wider interpretation of the past in question.

There are many other ways a history teacher might make use of

It Happened One Night. For example, students might be asked to investigate how the film actually was received in their own community. This might involve a trip to the local library to find newspaper reviews from that time. In some communities students might be able to locate the very theater in which the film originally was shown. Such activities exercise the studying competency involving "the ability to locate and use resources external to the classroom." They also take a further step toward inserting the film into its historical context. Locating the theater could lead students to some interesting investigations of neighborhoods and the nature of audiences in their own local history. This could also result in an oral history project in which students interview actual members of those audiences and inquire into what the local theater and the films of the time meant for them.

Many teachers will have sensed, however, that by the time students have considered the film at this length the limits of many high school students' endurance would have been reached. We understand this, and believe that teachers should stretch their students' attention but not exhaust it. Our extended discussion of this single film was intended not only to show how exercising many competencies can strengthen students' historical understanding but also to make a final point about studying in preparation for college. Explication of Ellie Andrews' experiences in problem recognition and problem solving may help students reflect on and improve their own approach to problems. Similarly, asking students to view the entire film another time will help prepare them for an important aspect of collegiate study. Although many high school social studies teachers feel required to move from one topic to another very quickly, the fact is that college students are expected to return to a topic or a text more than once, to work with it so as to attain a more than superficial understanding. Indeed, some psychologists believe that this ability to carry out sustained work and projects is a crucial dimension of developed intelligence. High school students need to be prepared in this sort of work.

VI. Toward Further Discussion

An independent, nationwide survey of teachers' attitudes indicates that the majority of teachers feel less than enthusiastic about recent educational reform measures enacted in their states.[1] This is not surprising given that the same poll indicates only 37 percent of the elementary and secondary teachers sampled felt they had been consulted in any way about these reform actions. The failure to include teachers at the very center of reform activities is, of course, a sure prescription for losing the current chance for improvement in education. As we pointed out in Chapter 2, it is unreasonable to expect that teachers can implement new curricula with conviction if their design does not incorporate teacher knowledge of subject matter and experience in how this knowledge can be transmitted to students through good teaching practice. The agenda for the immediate future must focus on ways to emphasize teachers' central role and responsibility in shaping excellent educational opportunities for all students. If we do not succeed in making this a matter of primary importance, the current reform impetus will be either seriously weakened or lost altogether.

Including teachers in major academic judgments and decisions involves reversing a stubborn historical trend. Diane Ravitch points out that the tendency during most of this century has been toward an increasing division between educational policymakers, on the one hand, and the teachers who are asked to carry out these policies in their classroom practice.[2] To end this separation, all concerned must seek to respect and rely upon one another's professionalism. Administrators and teachers must meet much more as colleagues, much less as supervisors and subordinates. Professional respect

---

1. *Education Week*, September 18, 1985.

2. Diane Ravitch, *The Schools We Deserve: Reflections on the Educational Crises of Our Times* (New York: Basic Books, 1985), p. 19.

involves better pay and better conditions for teachers; but it also means reliance on teachers' expert knowledge and experience in the design of curricula and learning programs. To make good educational policies we must start with what makes good sense in the classroom.

Professionalism for social studies teachers begins with strong preparation in an appropriate discipline and grows through using classroom experience to increase understanding of how knowledge and skills can be effectively transmitted to students. Moreover, teachers must remain learners themselves. We know that the most effective teachers are those who remain actively engaged learners in their own disciplines. This connection between good teaching and continued learning is partly a matter of being up-to-date in one's field, but perhaps has to do equally with keeping alive within oneself the feeling of being a student. This involves remaining sensitive to the difficulties as well as the satisfactions of learning, the labor as well as the achievement. Continued education in our own subject, that is, helps keep our knowledge vital and our feelings alert to both the opportunities and obstacles in the learning activities we undertake with students.

High School–College Collaboration

There are a variety of ways in which teachers can continue their learning, but we particularly recommend, along with our colleagues in several other subject areas, that this need be addressed through the development of new approaches to high school–college collaboration. In a large sense, such collaboration promises that an ongoing sharing of knowledge among colleagues in higher and secondary education can be applied to the creation of a coherent continuum of learning for students. We know that good education depends upon sustained effort, beginning very early in a child's life and involving parents, teachers, peers, and the community. Schooling informs this effort most effectively when it regards all study as of a piece, and makes connected use of the time available at successive levels of the entire educational process. In this view, the different educational levels and institutions are not discrete and separable compartments but rather related parts of a whole.

The challenge has been to fashion this continuum of learning in an educational system as large and varied as we find in our democracy. This book addresses only one part of the question—the successful negotiation for more students of the passage between high school and college. In offering suggestions, we have sought to call attention to the unity of what students need to know and be able to do in order to take good advantage of learning opportunities in both secondary and higher education. Our statement has been developed through dialogue carried on among high school and college teachers, and we present it as a start toward a common agenda. Through discussion we have learned much from one another and, like our colleagues in English, have been brought to understand the importance of the recommendation urged by James R. Vivian in the following statement:

> There is, in my view, no more important recommendation in the Carnegie Foundation Special Report on *School and College* than the one—contained also in the Carnegie Report on *High School*—that calls for universities and schools to develop genuine partnerships based on the needs of schools as determined by their principals and teachers. Both aspects of that recommendation are essential: not only that universities and schools work together, but especially that those of us in higher education encourage our colleagues in schools to show us the ways we can marshal our resources to address their needs.[3]

Vivian writes with particular reference to the work of the Yale–New Haven Teachers Institute, an ongoing collaborative project in which secondary school teachers and university faculty join together to prepare curriculum units and pedagogical strategies for use in the New Haven Public Schools. The roots of this effort go back to 1970 when the Yale History Department assisted a number of New Haven social studies teachers in developing improved curricula for courses in American history, world area studies, and urban studies (for a full account see *Teaching in America: The Common Ground*).[4] This project and others like it affirm that the

---

3. James R. Vivian in *Teaching in America: The Common Ground* (New York: College Entrance Examination Board, 1985), p. 8.

4. *Teaching in America: The Common Ground* (New York: College Entrance Examination Board, 1985).

problems and missions of school and college are fundamentally intertwined. Colleges have a critical interest in the prior education of their students and college faculty cannot stand apart from their high school colleagues as the nation discusses, and seeks to implement, better ways to prepare students for a lifetime of learning. The fact is that many high school teachers hear from their colleagues in higher education only through hearsay or from stories their former students bring to them about what is said and done in college classrooms. This obviously is not an adequate basis for what clearly must be a common endeavor.

We need, then, to create many more working partnerships of college and school faculties that center on the what and how of teaching. Such partnerships are needed at other levels as well—between high school and middle school teachers, for example. Given different local or regional conditions, such undertakings might take a variety of forms and adopt different practices. Nevertheless, discussion of any joint endeavor of this kind could benefit from consideration of the four principles that have guided the Yale–New Haven effort since its beginning: (1) a belief in the fundamental importance of the classroom teacher and of teacher-developed materials for effective learning; (2) an insistence that teachers of students at different levels interact as colleagues, addressing common problems of teaching their disciplines; (3) the conviction that any effort to improve teaching must be "teacher-centered"; and (4) a certainty that colleges can assist in improving schools only if they make a significant and long-term commitment to do so.

The Yale–New Haven Teachers Institute is only one of several encouraging signs in the area of high school–college collaboration. Sometimes, college faculty in history and the social sciences are charged with being interested solely in research and in specialized courses directly related to such research. Now, however, we sense a resurgence of interest in the broader pedagogical implications of new scholarship and an increased awareness among college faculty that the quality of work in their own classrooms depends on prior work in the schools. For the teaching of history, this may point to a welcome resumption of the legacy left by such scholars as Carl L. Becker, Charles Homer Haskins, and Frederick Jackson Turner. These historians and other distinguished colleagues helped establish history as a teaching as well as a research profession and all, as Hazel Hertzberg points out, were "involved in school history, as well as history in the colleges and universities."[5]

At the college level, the expertise in history and the social sciences needed to inform collaboration is not confined to a few centers of learning. Kammen points out, for example, that the profession of history "is no longer dominated by the history departments at a few prestigious universities. First-rate scholars are to be found throughout the country."[6] The same is true for the social sciences. What we need then to marshal these resources is a set of policies that calls attention to the important benefits of collaboration and provides rewards for faculty who participate.

There are many problems in the teaching of social studies that would benefit from collaborative discussion and effort. Three of the most important are the following.

Synthesis

Course organization in social studies at the high school level requires a synthesis of staggering amounts of material. Whereas college teachers and scholars sometimes take a specialized approach to subject matter, high school teachers must arrange long time-periods and a variety of topics into a coherent whole. The appropriate use of textbooks can help in this task, but there always remains a considerable time lag between the appearance of important new emphases or interpretations and their assimilation into textbook accounts. Ongoing exchange between college and high school teachers about substantive issues can help reduce this gap significantly, but such discussion is most useful when it includes attention to the pedagogical implications of new scholarship and, particularly, to the problems of incorporating growing, many-sided knowledge into course frameworks that convey a coherent, if not unitary, vision of past and present.

Currently, we need to give special attention to how the many new

---

5. Hazel W. Hertzberg, "The Teaching of History." In Michael Kammen (ed.), *The Past Before Us: Contemporary Historical Writing in the United States* (Ithaca, New York: Cornell University Press, 1980), p. 478.

6. Michael Kammen (ed.), "Introduction: The Historian's Vocation and the State of the Discipline in the United States," in *The Past Before Us*, p. 26.

findings in social history can vigorously inform the organization of courses in United States history and politics. We have discussed throughout this book how recent scholarship has vastly increased our historical awareness of groups formerly excluded, or slighted, in traditional historical narratives. This has increased knowledge of parts and aspects of society, but some argue that it has left us with an uncertain picture of the whole. As a result, we now hear a call "to pull together the vast mountain of scholarship produced in the past quarter century and make of it a coherent and explanatory account of American life."[7]

Attempting such a synthesis is a large task, and some scholars feel that it is neither doable nor appropriate. Others, however, believe that it is important to move in this direction and urge that we are on the verge of a new, large understanding of the American past. Even the beginnings of such an account could guide course development in school history, and perhaps lead particularly to what Kessner describes as "the emergence of a new political history deeply informed by social and cultural history."[8] This new approach to political life, it is argued, should embrace the public and civic life of all citizens, including "subordinate groups," and also explore the relations among these groups and their relation to the making of public life. We then would have a new perspective from which to study the ". . . civic arena where groups interact, even compete, to establish the configuration of political power in a society and its cultural forms and their meanings."[9]

Still, very difficult questions must be addressed. Some ask how a past that has been shown to be complex and various can now be seen as of a single piece. Might not the call for "synthesis" be a way of excluding many parts of the past—and moreover important parts—that cannot be made to fit? And would emphasis on "public life" return us again to a political history focusing on elites in disregard of all that we know about the deep political importance of social and economic processes? These are only a few of the questions that any attempt to construct a new synthesis must meet.

---

7. Thomas Kessner, *The New York Times*, October 6, 1985.

8. Ibid.

9. Ibid.

What we propose here is that such issues be joined not just in scholarly articles and monographs, but also in discussion among teachers about how we survey American history with our high school students. All things considered, the arena of school history may be where the question of synthesis is at once most important and most charged with controversy.

Questioning

The need for synthesis and coherent course organization does not suggest, however, that all connections must be made, or all uncertainties resolved, before work in the classroom can begin. Students must share in the recognition that definite answers to important questions often remain elusive and that this need not be an obstacle to study. Indeed, we have emphasized throughout this book that effective teaching helps students to know that good questions can be as important in learning as correct answers. Frameworks of study in which explanations seem too convenient or answers too pat do not encourage and develop critical thought.

Good teaching often begins with good questions and both college and high school teachers could benefit from more practice in their preparation and use. Teachers, after all, model the questioning spirit for students. Our questions shape and give direction to class discussions, tests, projects, and reports; and it is from these things that students often start when they begin to ask their own questions. Good questions also are the means through which we avoid creating a seeming (but false) division between skills and knowledge, competence and content. They engage content and, in doing so, elicit from students the exercise of skills that build academic competence. We want to underline once again the importance of providing this active, challenging experience to *all* students. Observation suggests that sometimes, even frequently, we share our questions only with a few. Benjamin Bloom reports that:

> Observations of teacher interaction with students in the classroom reveal that teachers frequently direct their teaching and explanation to some students and ignore others. They give much positive reinforcement and encouragement to some students but not to others, and they encourage active participating in the classroom from some students and discourage it from others. The studies find that typically teachers give

students in the top third of the class the greatest attention and students in the bottom third of the class receive the least attention and support.[10]

Such findings may come as no surprise and yet fail to seem relevant to one's own teaching. It is difficult, of course, to watch oneself teach. We fail to notice, perhaps, how often we look to the student who can help things along instead of seeking out the student who most needs our help. Where this is the case we need to find ways to change. Students regarded as low achievers deserve not only full support and encouragement but also the same opportunity to deal with imaginative, challenging questions as their high-achieving counterparts receive. If students in difficulty are excused from responding to questions, they are, in consequence, denied our most effective teaching. We must therefore find ways to look at our own teaching from the dual perspective of equity and quality. We should reflect on and analyze the questions that we ask different students. Is it the case that we direct our most interesting and significant questions to students who we anticipate will give a higher order of response? If we cannot be sure, there are several simple measures to consider.

- Arrange for a videotaping of our classes and analyze our teaching from the point of view of equitable interaction with all students. If technical assistance is not available, ask a trusted and experienced colleague to observe and provide feedback.
- Establish goals for involvement of all students. Maintain a seating chart of the class on which can be marked how often each student asked a question. Inform students in advance that you will seek even distribution of the marks made on the chart. Remind students, however, that each person has a responsibility not just for his or her own learning, but also for that of the class as a whole. This involves attentive listening as well as clear speaking in class discussion. Encourage listening skills by asking one student to add to or elaborate upon what another has said. Prepare selected questions to address to the entire class. Ask each student to write for two or three minutes in response to such questions

---

10. Benjamin Bloom (ed.), *Taxonomy of Educational Objectives, Handbook I: Cognitive Domain* (New York: David McKay, 1967), p. 11.

before asking individual students to read or speak about what they have written. Here again, encourage listening skills by asking students to place their remarks in the context of what other students have said.

- Have patience in building student competence through questioning. Students who rarely have been asked challenging questions will probably have little skill or interest in answering them: they and we can easily become discouraged. We must remember that competence comes slowly and that silence seldom means that nothing is happening. Experience indicates that the determination to ask is finally repaid by an equal determination to answer.

- Seek to have students frame and ask their own questions. If students rely entirely on questions asked by teachers, they will remain dependent learners. The ultimate purpose of the teacher is to encourage students to become independent learners. Students become independent—and thus responsible—to the extent that they formulate significant questions for which they desire to have answers.

Computers and Mathematics

More and more high schools are acquiring computers for use by their students. While this development raises serious equity issues concerning who has access to computers and for what purposes, there is no doubt that this new technology brings great promise. Our attitude toward computers is that they should be used for the unique and serious possibilities they bring to the social studies classroom. However, much currently available software is of the drill-and-practice variety, at a level of sophistication that would be embarrassing if the material were presented in a more familiar medium. Once the novelty wears off, schools may end up reconsidering their use of such software, much to their expensive chagrin. Much the same can be said of some simulation exercises where manipulation of variables is more elementary than what can be accomplished in routine student conversation. On the other hand, as pointed out in *Academic Preparation in English*, word processing can provide useful support to student writing, and writing is, of course, central to social studies learning. Beyond this use, it is true that computers are used in history and the social sciences to collect, retrieve, and statistically analyze large bodies of data. Indeed statistical analysis is at the heart of many of the social sciences. But this very fact raises important questions, not only about the use of computers, but also about the study of mathematics in high school.

In this book we have noted how quantitative information can change the questions we ask in the social studies. By comparing tallies and orders of magnitude students can generate interesting new questions or alter old ones in important ways. Indeed, the study of history would be more robust if teachers and students made more extensive use of what *Academic Preparation in Science* calls this comparative level of knowledge, transitional between qualitative and quantitative understanding. But the mathematics underlying these kinds of exercises is simply that of ratios, proportions, and percentages. Before schools leap to bring statistics into the social studies curriculum by means of computer software packages, it is worth considering a point emphasized in *Academic Preparation in Mathematics:* "Perhaps no other topics in mathematics surround and affect our lives as much and yet are so poorly understood as statistics and probability. . . . Yet in most high schools the mathematics curriculum gives only minimal attention to statistics." In short, statistics belongs in the high school curriculum but rarely can be found there. Understanding and use of statistics could bring a new seriousness to the high school study of many of the social sciences. Collaboration between mathematics and social studies teachers could even help secure the place of statistics in the high school curriculum. The crucial question, then, is not what computers can do but what use we are preparing our students to make of them. The important role that statistics could play in the social studies curriculum calls first, not for the purchase of expensive machines and software, but for further discussion and careful collaboration among teachers across disciplines and at all levels of education.

We know, of course, that our discussion in this chapter does not include all of the important academic issues facing social studies teachers. Our colleagues and readers will think of several others, some of which spring from local, rather than national, concerns. We hope, in fact, that what we have said will encourage others to add to the agenda we have begun to sketch throughout this book. Our aim has not been to establish this agenda, but to indicate the importance of making one—to take the chance offered by the current impetus toward educational reform to indicate what classroom initiatives teachers believe will benefit the great majority of our students. Moving forward with this agenda will require extensive collaboration among groups of faculty, administration, citizens, and elected and appointed officials; but no part of this working together is more essential, we believe than that needed between high school and college teachers in developing a genuine continuum of learning opportunities in the social studies.

Bibliography

Alder, Douglas D., and Matthew T. Downey. "Problem Areas in the History Curriculum." In Matthew T. Downey (ed.), *History in the Schools*. Washington, D.C.: National Council for the Social Studies, 1985.

Allen, Jack (ed.). *Education in the 80s: The Social Studies*. Washington, D.C.: National Education Association, 1981.

Annals of America, The, 19 vols. Chicago: Encyclopaedia Britannica, Inc., 1974,

Ballard, Martin (ed.). *New Movements in the Study and Teaching of History*. Bloomington, Indiana: Indiana University Press, 1970.

Banks, James A. *Teaching Strategies for Ethnic Studies*, 3rd ed. Boston: Allyn and Bacon, 1984.

Banks, James A., with Ambrose A. Clegg. *Teaching Strategies for the Social Studies: Inquiry, Valuing, and Decision Making*, 3rd ed. New York: Longman, 1985.

Barr, Robert D., James L. Barth, and S. Samuel Shermis. *Defining the Social Studies*. Washington, D.C.: National Council for the Social Studies, 1977.

Baxandall, Rosalyn, Linda Gordon, and Susan Reverby. *America's Working Women: A Documentary History—1600 to the Present*. New York: Random House, 1976.

Becker, Carl. *Everyman His Own Historian*. Chicago: Quadrangle Books, 1966.

Berger, Peter, Brigitte Berger, and Hansfried Kellner. *The Homeless Mind: Modernization and Consciousness*. New York: Random House, 1973.

Berkin, Carol, and Leonard Wood. *Land of Promise: A History of the United States from 1865*. Glenview, Illinois: Scott, Foresman, 1983.

Berry, Mary Francis, and John W. Blassingame. *Long Memory: The Black Experience in America*. New York: Oxford University Press, 1982.

Black, C. E. *The Dynamics of Modernization: A Study in Comparative History*. New York: Harper & Row, 1967.

Bloom, Benjamin (ed.). *Taxonomy of Educational Objectives, Handbook I: Cognitive Domain*. New York: David McKay, 1967.

Cartwright, William H., and Richard L. Watson, Jr. (eds.). *The Reinterpretation of American History and Culture*. Washington, D.C.: National Council for the Social Studies, 1973.

Colbourn, Trevor, and James T. Patterson (eds.). *The American Past in Perspective*. Vol. 2, *Since 1865*. Boston: Allyn and Bacon, 1970.

College Board, The. *Teaching in America: The Common Ground*. New York: College Entrance Examination Board, 1985.

Commager, Henry Steele (ed.). *Documents of American History*, 9th ed., 2 vols. Englewood Cliffs, New Jersey: Prentice-Hall, 1973.

Coser, Lewis A. *Masters of Sociological Thought: Ideas in Historical and Social Context*, 2nd ed. New York: Harcourt Brace Jovanovich, 1977.

Cott, Nancy F. (ed.). *Root of Bitterness: Documents of the Social History of American Women*. New York: Dutton, 1972.

Cross, Robert D. "American Society: 1865-1914." In John A. Garraty (ed.), *Interpreting American History: Conversations with Historians, Part II*. New York: Macmillan, 1970.

Darnton, Robert. "Intellectual and Cultural History." In Michael Kammen (ed.), *The Past Before Us: Contemporary Historical Writing in the United States*. Ithaca, New York: Cornell University Press, 1980.

Diamond, Sigmund. "The European Basis of American Civilization." In John A. Garraty (ed.), *Interpreting American History: Conversations with Historians, Part I*. New York: Macmillan, 1970.

Dinnerstein, Leonard, and Frederic Cople Jaher (eds.). *The Aliens: A History of Ethnic Minorities in America*. New York: Appleton-Century-Crofts, 1970.

Downey, Matthew T. (ed.). *History in the Schools*. Washington, D.C.: National Council for the Social Studies, 1985.

Downey, Matthew T. (ed.). *Teaching American History: New Directions*. Washington, D.C.: National Council for the Social Studies, 1982.

Du Bois, W. E. B. *The Souls of Black Folk*. New York: New American Library, 1969.

Ellison, Ralph. "Hidden Name and Complex Fate." In *Shadow and Act*. New York: New American Library, 1966.

Engle, Shirley H. (ed.). *New Perspectives in World History*, 34th yearbook. Washington, D.C.: National Council for the Social Studies, 1964.

Ethnic and Immigration Groups: The United States, Canada, and England. Institute for Research in History. New York: Haworth, 1983.

Fitzgibbon, Russel H., and Julio A. Fernandez. *Latin America: Political Culture and Development*, 2nd ed. Englewood Cliffs, New Jersey: Prentice-Hall, 1981.

Garraty, John A. (ed.). *Interpreting American History: Conversations with Historians, Parts I and II*. New York: Macmillan, 1970.

Garraty, John A., and Peter Gay (eds.). *The Columbia History of the World*. New York: Harper & Row, 1981, 1983.

Harding, Vincent. *There Is a River: The Black Struggle for Freedom in America*. New York: Vintage, 1981.

Hertzberg, Hazel W. "Students, Methods and Materials of Instruction." In Matthew T. Downey (ed.), *History in the Schools*. Washington, D.C.: National Council for the Social Studies, 1985.

————. "The Teaching of History." In Michael Kammen (ed.), *The Past Before Us: Contemporary Historical Writing in the United States*. Ithaca, New York: Cornell University Press, 1980.

History Teacher, The. Society for History Education, Department of History, California State University, Long Beach, 1250 Bellflower Blvd., Long Beach, California 90840.

Huizinga, J. "Historical Conceptualization." In Fritz Stern (ed.), *The Varieties of History from Voltaire to the Present*. Cleveland, Ohio: World Publishing, 1956.

Hymowitz, Carol, and Michaele Weissman. *A History of Women in America*. New York: Bantam Books, 1978.

Intercom. Global Perspectives in Education, 218 East 18th Street, New York, New York 10003.

Jones, Maldwyn Allen. "The Impact of Immigration." In Trevor Colbourn and James T. Patterson (eds.), *The American Past in Perspective*. Vol. 2, *Since 1865*. Boston: Allyn and Bacon, 1970.

Joyce, James. *Dubliners*. Harmondsworth, Middlesex: Penguin Books, 1956.

Kammen, Michael (ed.). *The Past Before Us: Contemporary Historical Writing in the United States*. Ithaca, New York: Cornell University Press, 1980.

Katz, Stanley N., and Stanley I. Kutler (eds.). *New Perspectives on the American Past*. Vol. 2, *1877 to the Present*. Boston: Little, Brown, 1969.

Krug, Mark M. *History and the Social Sciences: New Approaches to the Teaching of Social Studies*. Waltham, Massachusetts: Blaisdell, 1967.

Kuhn, Thomas S. *The Structure of Scientific Revolutions*, 2nd ed., enlarged. Chicago: University of Chicago Press, 1970.

Lamar, Howard R. "Encounter with a City: Education and the Promise of Local History." In *Teaching in America: The Common Ground*. New York: College Entrance Examination Board, 1985.

Langer, William L. (compiler and ed.). *An Encyclopedia of World History*, 5th ed. Boston: Houghton Mifflin, 1972.

Lerner, Gerda (ed.). *Black Women in White America: A Documentary History*. New York: Vintage Books, 1973.

Linder, Bertram L., and Edwin Selzer (eds.). "Teaching about World History in the Cities." *Social Education* 46 (March 1982): 176-199.

McNeill, William H. *The Rise of the West: A History of the Human Community.* Chicago: University of Chicago Press, 1970.

McNeill, William H. *A World History,* 3rd ed. New York: Oxford University Press, 1970.

McNeill, William H., and Jean W. Sedlar (eds.). *Readings in World History.* New York: Oxford University Press, 1968 to 1973.

McNeill, William H., et al. "Beyond Western Civilization: Rebuilding the Survey." *The History Teacher* 10 (August 1977): 509-548.

Mehlinger, Howard, and O. L. Davis (eds.). *The Social Studies,* 80th yearbook of the National Society for the Study of Education. Chicago: University of Chicago Press, 1981.

Morison, Samuel Eliot, Henry Steele Commager, and William E. Leuchtenburg. *The Growth of the American Republic,* 2 vols. New York: Oxford University Press, 1969.

Morris, Richard B. *The U.S. Department of Labor Bicentennial History of the American Worker.* Washington, D.C.: U.S. Government Printing Office, 1976.

Morris, Richard B., and Jeffrey B. Morris (eds.). *Encyclopedia of American History.* New York: Harper & Row, 1976.

Muessig, Raymond H. (ed.). *The Study and Teaching of Social Science Series,* 6 vols. Columbus, Ohio: Merrill, 1980.

Negro History Bulletin. Association for the Study of Negro Life and History, 1401 Fourteenth Street N.W., Washington, D.C. 20005.

Newmann, Fred M. *Education for Citizen Action: Challenge for Secondary Curriculum.* Berkeley, California: McCutchan, 1975.

Osborn, Richard, et al. "Revision of the NCSS Social Studies Curriculum Guidelines." *Social Education* 43 (April 1979): 261-278.

Project SPAN Staff and Consultants. *The Current State of the Social Studies: A Report of Project SPAN.* Boulder, Colorado: Social Science Education Consortium, 1982.

Pycior, Julie Leininger. "Acculturation and Pluralism in Recent Studies of American Immigration History." In *Ethnic and Immigration Groups: The United States, Canada, and England.* Institute for Research in History. New York: Haworth, 1983.

Ravitch, Diane. *The Schools We Deserve: Reflections on the Educational Crises of Our Times.* New York: Basic Books, 1985.

Rodgers, Richard, and Oscar Hammerstein II. "The King and I." In *6 Plays by Rodgers and Hammerstein.* New York: Random House, 1959.

Rosenzweig, Linda W. (ed.). "Teaching about Social History." *Social Education* 48 (May 1982): 321-336.

Shaftel, Fannie R., and George Shaftel. *Role Playing in the Curriculum,* 2nd ed. Englewood Cliffs, New Jersey: Prentice-Hall, 1982.

Sitton, Thad, George L. Mehaffy, and O. L. Davis, Jr. *Oral History: A*

Guide for Teachers (and Others). Austin, Texas: University of Texas Press, 1983.

Social Education. National Council for the Social Studies, 3501 Newark Street, Washington, D.C. 20016.

Social Studies, The. Heldref Publications, 4000 Albemarle Street, Washington, D.C. 20016.

Stern, Fritz (ed.). *The Varieties of History from Voltaire to the Present.* Cleveland, Ohio: World Publishing, 1956.

Sussman, Warren. *Culture as History: The Transformation of American Society in the Twentieth Century.* New York: Pantheon Books, 1984.

"Teaching about American Labor History." *Social Education* 45 (February 1982): 92-109.

Teaching History: A Journal of Methods. Division of Social Sciences, Emporia State University, Emporia, Kansas 66801.

Terkel, Studs. *American Dreams: Lost and Found.* New York: Pantheon Books, 1980.

Theodorson, George A., and Achilles G. Theodorson. *A Modern Dictionary of Sociology.* New York: Thomas Y. Crowell, 1969.

Thistlethwaite, Frank. "Migration from Europe Overseas in the Nineteenth and Twentieth Centuries." In Stanley N. Katz and Stanley I. Kutler (eds.), *New Perspectives on the American Past.* Vol. 2, *1877 to the Present.* Boston: Little, Brown, 1969.

Thompson, Edward P. *The Making of the English Working Class.* New York: Random House, 1966.

Turner, Frederick Jackson. "An American Definition of History." In Fritz Stern (ed.), *The Varieties of History from Voltaire to the Present.* Cleveland, Ohio: World Publishing, 1956.

White, Theodore H. *In Search of History: A Personal Adventure.* New York: Warner Books, 1978.

Whitehead, Alfred North. *The Aims of Education and Other Essays.* New York: New American Library, 1949.

Wood, Jayne Miller. "Adding a Global Outlook to Our Secondary Curriculum: Classroom Teaching Strategies." *Social Education* 38 (November-December 1974): 664-671.

Appendix A. Social Studies

Why?

The social studies focus on the complexity of our social environment. The subject combines the study of history and the social sciences and promotes skills in citizenship.

We live in a distinct kind of society and all people need to understand how such modern societies function and how they have developed. They need information concerning past civilizations and their links to present ones.

If people are to perform effectively as citizens in a democratic society, they need knowledge about central institutions and values in their own society and in other major societies around the world. They need to understand the international context of contemporary life. Defining problems and employing various kinds of information in seeking solutions to those problems require the analytical skills developed in the study of history and the social sciences.

Preparation in social studies will be important to college entrants in other ways. It will help them understand major and exciting discoveries about human beings and their social environment as well as the practical results of these discoveries. It will help them understand the context for the arts and sciences. It will help them prepare for advanced work in history and the social sciences, including anthropology, economics, geography, political science, psychology, and sociology.

What?

All college entrants will need the following general understanding of the social studies.

- Basic factual knowledge of major political and economic institutions and their historical development.
- Basic factual knowledge of the social and cultural fields of history.
- An introductory knowledge of the content and concepts of the social sciences.

- A grasp of major trends in the contemporary world (for example, nationalism or urbanization).
- Familiarity with a variety of written, numerical, and visual forms of data.
- Familiarity with the techniques of quantitative and nonquantitative analysis.
- Familiarity with diverse interpretations of data.

History

College entrants will need certain general knowledge and skills in political, social, and cultural history.

- Some understanding of the relationship between present and past, including contrasts between contemporary institutions and values and those of the past, the reasons for these contrasts, and leading continuities between past and present.
- Some understanding of how to approach the problem of change over time.
- The ability to recognize historical cause and effect.
- The ability to identify major historical turning points.
- Some ability to develop historical interpretations.

More specifically, college entrants will need the following basic knowledge.

World History, Geography and Cultures

- The basic features of major societies and cultures in the contemporary world: their geography, major economic and social structures, political systems, and religions.
- The historical developments underlying present connections and similarities among the world's peoples, and the major differences dividing them.
- The chronology and significance of major events and movements in world history (for example, the Renaissance, the Industrial Revolution, and the spread of Islam).
- The international context of contemporary diplomacy and economics.

United States History

- The relationship between events and historical trends in the United States and trends elsewhere in the world, developed through analysis of major similarities and differences.

- The interaction among peoples of different national origins, races, and cultures, and how such interaction has shaped American history.
- The chronology and impact of political events, development of governmental and other social institutions, technological and environmental changes, and changes in social and cultural values.

Social Science

College entrants will need the following basic knowledge and skills in the social sciences.

- The ability to understand basic information developed by the social sciences, including statistical data and other materials.
- Familiarity with the basic method of the social sciences, that is, with the framing and empirical testing of hypotheses.
- A basic understanding of at least one of the social sciences and of how its practitioners define and solve problems.
- Familiarity with how to explore a social problem or social institution by means of ideas drawn from several social sciences.

Appendix B. Eveline

She sat at the window watching the evening invade the avenue. Her head was leaned against the window curtains, and in her nostrils was the odour of dusty cretonne. She was tired.

Few people passed. The man out of the last house passed on his way home; she heard his footsteps clacking along the concrete pavement and afterwards crunching on the cinder path before the new red houses. One time there used to be a field there in which they used to play every evening with other people's children. Then a man from Belfast bought the field and built houses in it—not like their little brown houses, but bright brick houses with shining roofs. The children of the avenue used to play together in that field—the Devines, the Waters, the Dunns, little Keogh the cripple, she and her brothers and sisters. Ernest, however, never played: he was too grown up. Her father used often to hunt them in out of the field with his blackthorn stick; but usually little Keogh used to keep *nix* and call out when he saw her father coming. Still they seemed to have been rather happy then. Her father was not so bad then; and besides, her mother was alive. That was a long time ago; she and her brothers and sisters were all grown up; her mother was dead. Tizzie Dunn was dead, too, and the Waters had gone back to England. Everything changes. Now she was going to go away like the others, to leave her home.

Home! She looked round the room, reviewing all its familiar objects which she had dusted once a week for so many years, wondering where on earth all the dust came from. Perhaps she would never see again those familiar objects from which she had never dreamed of being divided. And yet during all those years she had never found out the name of the priest whose yellowing photograph hung on the wall above the broken harmonium beside the coloured print of the promises made to Blessed Margaret Mary Alacoque. He had been a school friend of her father. Whenever he showed the photograph to a visitor her father used to pass it with a casual word:

'He is in Melbourne now.'

She had consented to go away, to leave her home. Was that wise? She tried to weigh each side of the question. In her home anyway she had shelter and food; she had those whom she had known all her life about her. Of course she had to work hard, both in the house and at business. What would they say of her in the Stores when they found out that she had run away with a fellow? Say she was a fool, perhaps; and her place would be filled up by advertisement. Miss Gavan would be glad. She had always had an edge on her, especially whenever there were people listening.

'Miss Hill, don't you see these ladies are waiting?'

'Look lively, Miss Hill, please.'

She would not cry many tears at leaving the Stores.

But in her new home, in a distant unknown country, it would not be like that. Then she would be married—she, Eveline. People would treat her with respect then. She would not be treated as her mother had been. Even now, though she was over nineteen, she sometimes felt herself in danger of her father's violence. She knew it was that that had given her the palpitations. When they were growing up he had never gone for her, like he used to go for Harry and Ernest, because she was a girl; but latterly he had begun to threaten her and say what he would do to her only for her dead mother's sake. And now she had nobody to protect her. Ernest was dead and Harry, who was in the church decorating business, was nearly always down somewhere in the country. Besides, the invariable squabble for money on Saturday nights had begun to weary her unspeakably. She always gave her entire wages—seven shillings—and Harry always sent up what he could, but the trouble was to get any money from her father. He said she used to squander the money, that she had no head, that he wasn't going to give her his hard-earned money to throw about the streets, and much more, for he was usually fairly bad on Saturday night. In the end he would give her the money and ask her had she any intention of buying Sunday's dinner. Then she had to rush out as quickly as she could and do her marketing, holding her black leather purse tightly in her hand as she elbowed her way through the crowds and returning home late under her load of provisions. She had hard work to keep the house together and see that the two young children who had been left to her charge went to school regularly and got their meals regularly. It was hard work—a hard life—but now that she was about to leave it she did not find it a wholly undesirable life.

She was about to explore another life with Frank. Frank was very kind, manly, open-hearted. She was to go away with him by the night-boat to be his wife and to live with him in Buenos Ayres, where he had a home waiting for her. How well she remembered the first time she had seen him; he was lodging in a house on the main road where she used to visit. It seemed a few weeks ago. He was standing at the gate, his peaked cap pushed back on his head and his hair tumbled forward over a face of bronze. Then they had come to know each other. He used to meet her outside the Stores every evening and see her home. He took her to see *The Bohemian Girl* and she felt elated as she sat in an unaccustomed part of the theatre with him. He was awfully fond of music and sang a little. People knew that they were courting, and, when he sang about the lass that loves a sailor, she always felt pleasantly confused. He used to call her Poppens out of fun. First of all it had been an excitement for her to have a fellow and then she had begun to like him. He had tales of distant countries. He had started as a deck boy at a pound a month on a ship of the Allan Line going out to Canada. He told her the names of the ships he had been on and the names of the different services. He had sailed through the Straits of Magellan and he told her stories of the terrible Patagonians. He had fallen on his feet in Buenos Ayres, he said, and had come over to the old country just for a holiday. Of course, her father had found out the affair and had forbidden her to have anything to say to him.

'I know these sailor chaps,' he said.

One day he had quarrelled with Frank, and after that she had to meet her lover secretly.

The evening deepened in the avenue. The white of two letters in her lap grew indistinct. One was to Harry; the other was to her father. Ernest had been her favourite, but she liked Harry too. Her father was becoming old lately, she noticed; he would miss her. Sometimes he could be very nice. Not long before, when she had been laid up for a day, he had read her out a ghost story and made toast for her at the fire. Another day, when their mother was alive, they had all gone for a picnic to the Hill of Howth. She remembered her father putting on her mother's bonnet to make the children laugh.

Her time was running out, but she continued to sit by the window, leaning her head against the window curtain, inhaling the odour of dusty cretonne. Down far in the avenue she could hear a street organ playing. She knew the air. Strange that it should come that very night to remind her of the promise to her mother, her promise to keep the home together as long as she could. She remembered the last night of her mother's illness; she was again in the close, dark room at the other side of the hall and outside she heard a melancholy air of Italy. The organ-player had been ordered to go away and given sixpence. She remembered her father strutting back into the sick-room saying:

'Damned Italians! coming over here!'

As she mused the pitiful vision of her mother's life laid its spell on the very quick of her being—that life of commonplace sacrifices closing in final craziness. She trembled as she heard again her mother's voice saying constantly with foolish insistence:

'Derevaun Seraun! Derevaun Seraun!'

She stood up in a sudden impulse of terror. Escape! She must escape! Frank would save her. He would give her life, perhaps love, too. But she wanted to live. Why should she be unhappy? She had a right to happiness. Frank would take her in his arms, fold her in his arms. He would save her.

*

She stood among the swaying crowd in the station at the North Wall. He held her hand and she knew that he was speaking to her, saying something about the passage over and over again. The station was full of soldiers with brown baggages. Through the wide doors of the sheds she caught a glimpse of the black mass of the boat, lying in beside the quay wall, with illumined portholes. She answered nothing. She felt her cheek pale and cold and, out of a maze of distress, she prayed to God to direct her, to show her what was her duty. The boat blew a long mournful whistle into the mist. If she went, to-morrow she would be on the sea with Frank, steaming towards Buenos Ayres. Their passage had been booked. Could she still draw back after all he had done for her? Her distress awoke a nausea in her body and she kept moving her lips in silent fervent prayer.

A bell clanged upon her heart. She felt him seize her hand:

'Come!'

All the seas of the world tumbled about her heart. He was drawing her into them: he would drown her. She gripped with both hands at the iron railing.

'Come!'

No! No! No! It was impossible. Her hands clutched the iron in frenzy. Amid the seas she sent a cry of anguish.

'Eveline! Evvy!'

He rushed beyond the barrier and called to her to follow. He was shouted at to go on, but he still called to her. She set her white face to him, passive, like a helpless animal. Her eyes gave him no sign of love or farewell or recognition.

Members of the Council on Academic Affairs, 1983-85

Peter N. Stearns, Heinz Professor of History, Carnegie-Mellon University, Pittsburgh, Pennsylvania (*Chair* 1983-85)

Dorothy S. Strong, Director of Mathematics, Chicago Public Schools, Illinois (*Vice Chair* 1983-85)

Victoria A. Arroyo, College Board Student Representative, Emory University, Atlanta, Georgia (1983-84)

Ida S. Baker, Principal, Cape Coral High School, Florida (1984-85)

Michael Anthony Brown, College Board Student Representative, University of Texas, Austin (1983-85)

Jean-Pierre Cauvin, Associate Professor of French, Department of French and Italian, University of Texas, Austin (1983-84)

Alice C. Cox, Assistant Vice President, Student Academic Services, Office of the President, University of California (1983-84, Trustee Liaison 1984-85)

Charles M. Dorn, Professor of Art and Design, Department of Creative Arts, Purdue University, West Lafayette, Indiana (1983-84)

Sidney H. Estes, Assistant Superintendent, Instructional Planning and Development, Atlanta Public Schools, Georgia (1983-85)

David B. Greene, Chairman, Division of Humanities, Wabash College, Crawfordsville, Indiana (1984-85)

Jan A. Guffin, Chairman, Department of English, North Central High School, Indianapolis, Indiana (1983-85)

John W. Kenelly, Professor of Mathematical Sciences, Clemson University, South Carolina (1983-85)

Mary E. Kesler, Assistant Headmistress, The Hockaday School, Dallas, Texas (Trustee Liaison 1983-85)

Arthur E. Levine, President, Bradford College, Massachusetts (1983-85)

Deirdre A. Ling, Vice Chancellor for University Relations and Development, University of Massachusetts, Amherst (Trustee Liaison 1983-84)

Judith A. Lozano-Loredo, Superintendent, Southside Independent School District, San Antonio, Texas (1983-84)